Faculty Status for Librarians

by

Virgil F. Massman

The Scarecrow Press, Inc.
Metuchen, N.J.   1972

TO NANCY

ACKNOWLEDGMENTS

Many people contributed to this study. To all I am most grateful.

I wish to express my appreciation to the librarians and faculty members who took the time to complete the questionnaires and to the many who wrote thoughtful comments; to Dr. Kenneth E. Vance, who read several versions of the dissertation and mace helpful suggestions on all of them; to the other members of the committee who were always available for consultation; to Elizabeth Thompson, who assisted in proofreading and indexing of the final copy for printing; to my wife Nancy, who typed many drafts without relish but without undue complaint; and to my children Samuel, Donna, and Ruth Ann, who did not help much but who wanted to.

CONTENTS

Page

Acknowledgments   iv

List of Tables   vi

Chapter

  1.   Introduction   1

Part I: Related Literature

  2.   The Question of Faculty or Academic Status?   11

  3.   Problems and Responsibilities of Faculty
         Status   43

  4.   Benefits of Faculty Status   85

Part II: The Survey

  5.   General Characteristics of the Respondents   112

  6.   Problems and Responsibilities of Faculty
         Status   126

  7.   Benefits of Faculty Status   155

  8.   Comments by Faculty Members and Librarians   183

  9.   General Summary and Conclusions   198

Selected Bibliography   212

Index   225

LIST OF TABLES

Table   Page

1   Selected Previous Surveys on the Academic or Faculty Status of Librarians   18

2   Highest Degrees of Academic Librarians as Shown in Selected Previous Studies   49

3   Highest Degrees of Librarians Reported in Theses and Dissertations   55

4   Percentage of Faculty Members with the Doctorate as Shown in Selected Previous Studies   57

5   Percentage of Full-Time Faculty Members with the Doctorate by Type of Institution in 1953-54 and in 1962-63   57

6   U.S. Census Figures on Male and Female Librarians   67

7   Percentage of Male and Female Librarians in Selected Previous Studies   69

8   Percentage of Male and Female Faculty Members in American Colleges and Universities as Reported in 1961   69

9   Eligibility of Librarians for Sabbatical Leaves in Selected Previous Studies   89

10   Salaries of Librarians and Faculty Members: 1910 and 1925   94

11   Percentage of Faculty Members with the Doctorate in Various Academic Ranks in American Colleges and Universities in 1953-54 and 1962-63   95

12   Median Salaries of Faculty Members in 1,017 Colleges and Universities in 1965-66   96

vi

Table   Page

13   Average Salaries of Faculty Members in 1965-66 in 14 Institutions Included in the Present Survey   97

14   Average Salaries of Librarians in 1965-66 in 14 Institutions Included in the Present Survey   97

15   Age of Librarians by Sex   114

16   Age of Faculty Members by Sex   114

17   Years of Experience as Librarians by Sex   116

18   Years of Experience as College Teachers of Faculty Members by Sex   116

19   Average Number of Years Librarians Have Been at Their Present Institutions   118

20   Average Number of Years Faculty Members Have Been at Their Present Institutions   118

21   Positions of Librarians by Sex   119

22   Supervision of Professional Staff by Librarians by Sex   121

23   Supervision of Non-Professional Staff by Librarians by Sex   121

24   Median Rankings of Ten Positions from 1 (Most) to 10 (Least Important) by Faculty Members by Sex   122

25   How Librarians Think Faculty Would Rank Ten Positions by Sex--Median Rankings from 1 (Most) to 10 (Least Important)   122

26   Median Rankings of Ten Positions from 1 (Most) to 10 (Least Important) by Librarians by Sex   123

27   Average Number of Hours Taught by Librarians   125

28   Average Number of Hours Taught by Faculty Members by Rank and Sex   125

29   Highest Degrees Held by Librarians by Sex   127

Table		Page
30	Advanced Degrees Expected by Librarians by Sex	128
31	Education of Head Librarians in 17 Institutions	129
32	Highest Degrees of Faculty Members by Sex	130
33	Average Number of Credits beyond Highest Degree Earned by Faculty Members	130
34	Advanced Degrees Expected by Faculty Members by Sex	131
35	Pressure to Work Toward the Doctorate by Librarians by Sex	132
36	Pressure to Work Toward the Doctorate by Faculty Members by Sex	132
37	Librarians' Recommendations for Minimal Degrees for Librarians by Sex	134
38	Faculty Recommendations for Minimal Degrees for Librarians by Sex	135
39	Librarians' Recommendations for Terminal Degrees for Librarians by Sex	136
40	Faculty Recommendations for Terminal Degrees for Librarians by Sex	137
41	Educational Attainments and Aspirations of Librarians and Faculty Members	139
42	Publications during the Past Two Years by Librarians by Sex	140
43	Publications during the Past Two Years by Faculty Members by Sex	141
44	Number of Librarians and Faculty Members Who Published during the Past Two Years	142
45	Faculty Members and Librarians as Voting Members of the Faculty	143
46	Eligibility for Election to the Faculty Senate and Current Membership in That Body by Librarians by Sex	144

Table		Page
47	Eligibility for Election to the Faculty Senate and Current Membership in That Body by Faculty Members by Sex	145
48	Eligibility for Election and Service on Academic Committees by Librarians by Sex	146
49	Eligibility for Election and Service on Academic Committees by Faculty Members by Sex	147
50	Number of Faculty Members and Librarians on a Selected Number of Committees	148
51	Membership in Professional Associations of Librarians by Sex	149
52	Membership in Professional Associations of Faculty Members by Sex	150
53	Membership on Committees and Offices Held in Professional Associations by Librarians by Sex	151
54	Membership on Committees and Offices Held in Professional Associations by Faculty Members by Sex	151
55	Membership of Librarians in Certain National Associations	153
56	Membership of Faculty Members in Certain National Associations	153
57	Academic Rank of Librarians by Sex	156
58	Academic Rank of Faculty Members by Sex	156
59	Academic Rank of Faculty Members with the Doctorate	157
60	Academic Rank of Librarians with the Doctorate	157
61	Sabbatical Leaves Received by Librarians by Sex	160
62	Sabbatical Leaves Received by Faculty Members by Sex	160

ix

Table		Page
63	Eligibility of Librarians for Sabbatical Leaves by Sex	161
64	Eligibility of Faculty Members for Sabbatical Leaves by Sex	161
65	Leaves of Absence Without Salary Taken by Librarians by Sex	163
66	Leaves of Absence Without Salary Taken by Faculty Members by Sex	163
67	Sabbaticals Received, Eligibility for Sabbaticals, and Leaves of Absence Taken by Librarians and Faculty Members	164
68	Average Salaries of Faculty Members and Librarians by Sex	165
69	Average Salaries of Librarians by Degrees and Sex	167
70	Average Salaries of Faculty Members by Degrees and Sex	167
71	Average Salaries of Faculty Members with the Master's as the Highest Degree Compared with Librarians with Two Master's Degrees, with the Sixth-Year Degree, and the Master's Degree	170
72	Average Salaries of Librarians by Rank and Sex	171
73	Average Salaries of Faculty Members by Rank and Sex	171
74	Average Salaries of Librarians Who Published During the Past Two Years by Sex	173
75	Average Salaries of Faculty Members Who Published during the Past Two Years by Sex	173
76	Eligibility for Tenure by Faculty Members and Librarians	174

x

Table		Page

Table		Page
77	Term of Contract of Librarians by Sex	175
78	Vacations of Librarians	176
79	Librarians Who Published During the Past Two Years by Term of Contract by Sex	177
80	Average Number of Items Published by Librarians during the Past Two Years by Term of Contract by Sex	177
81	Librarians Who Expect to Earn Another Degree by Term of Contract and Sex	177
82	Knowledge of Availability of Research Funds	179
83	Research Funds and Time for Research Requested and Received by Librarians by Sex	179
84	Research Funds and Time for Research Requested and Received by Faculty Members by Sex	180
85	Research Funds Received by Librarians and Faculty Members	180
86	Travel Funds Received by Librarians by Sex During the Past Year	181
87	Travel Funds Received by Faculty Members by Sex during the Past Year	182
88	Travel Funds Received by Librarians and Faculty Members during the Past Year	182

Chapter 1

INTRODUCTION

Academic librarians have been striving to achieve
faculty status for many years, and recently the desire for
such recognition has resulted in direct action by professional
library associations. At the annual convention of the American Library Association (ALA) at Atlantic City in June, 1969,
the Librarians Concerned about Academic Status introduced
a series of demands at the meeting of the Academic Status
Committee of the University Libraries Section.[1] This latter
group is a section of the Association of College and Research
Libraries (ACRL) which, in turn, is a division of ALA.
David Kaser, President of ACRL, later presented the Academic Status Committee's resolution to the ALA Council. The
resolution reads:

Whereas, academic librarians must have

1) Rank equivalent to other members of the teaching faculty;

2) Salary equal to that of other members of the
teaching faculty;

3) Sabbatical and other leaves;

4) Tenure;

5) Access to grants, fellowships, and research
funds;

6) Responsibilities for professional duties only;

7) An adequately supportive non-professional staff;

8) Appointment and promotion on the basis of individual accomplishment and involving peer
review;

1

9)   Grievance and appeal procedures available to
      other members of the academic community
      and involving peer review;

10)   Participation of all librarians in library
      governance;

11)   Membership in the academic senate of their
      institutions, or other governing bodies;

Therefore, be it RESOLVED: That the Association
of College and Research Libraries and the American Library Association adopt as their official policy
the support of these standards for all academic li-
librarians and the implementation of these standards
by any and all appropriate professional means, including: 1) censure and sanctions; 2) accreditation
of libraries. [2]

While the ALA membership had already voted on and approved
a resolution to adopt a policy to support professional standards for librarians, the accreditation of libraries, and the use
of censure and sanctions, [3] the ALA Council expressed its re-
sounding opposition to the ACRL resolution by a vote of 72 to
13.   Because the Executive Board of ACRL had anticipated a
negative vote from the Council, David Kaser then announced
that ACRL was planning to proceed independently of ALA. [4]

Particularly in the recent past, librarians have stressed
the benefits of faculty status as is shown by the ACRL resolution and the 1968 resolution of the California librarians. [5]
However, the faculty may expect the "standards of degrees
and professional competence of librarians recruited to be
equivalent to those applied to professors" and maintain that
promotion must be "based on merit, applying standards, criteria, and procedures equivalent to those used for professors."[6] Thus when librarians argue for full faculty status,
the faculty may express concern about standards for appointment and promotion.

Need for the Study

Although many articles have been written on faculty
status for librarians and a number of surveys have been done
on existing conditions, little precise information is available
on how librarians actually compare with faculty members in
regard to education, research and writing, service on aca-

demic committees, professional activity, etc. The ACRL
resolution asserts that librarians must have "rank equivalent
to other members of the teaching faculty" and "salary equal
to that of other members of the teaching faculty." Equal on
what basis? The argument seems to be that the two groups
are comparable, but no one has analyzed the similarities or
differences in detail.

It does not seem appropriate nor particularly mean-
ingful to contrast salaries of librarians and faculty members
without taking into consideration possible disparities in such
critical areas as degrees, publications, service on academic
committees, and professional activity. If librarians are to
make comparisons, they must do so on the basis of information derived from existing conditions. This is all the more
important in view of the growing agitation by librarians for
full and formal faculty status. On the other hand, the benefits of faculty status such as sabbaticals, equal salary, tenure, faculty rank, access to research funds, and travel funds
are important factors in encouraging librarians to meet faculty standards. Both the benefits and the responsibilities
of faculty status should be of concern to academic librarians.
However, existing conditions have not been subjected to intensive research. As will be shown later, academic librarians have not even reached an agreement on the fundamental
issue of what constitutes academic or faculty status, and
terms have often been used interchangeably. Such lack of
precision helps little to resolve the issue.

Purpose

        Briefly stated, the purpose of this study is: (1) to
review the history of the struggle for faculty status for librarians and some of the arguments advanced in support of
that objective; and (2) to gather information on the similarities and differences between librarians and faculty members
in the broad areas of preparation, contributions, and rewards. With detailed information on such matters as education, salaries, professional experience, tenure, sabbaticals,
participation in academic government, and scholarly activity
of librarians and faculty members, one should be able to
judge whether librarians receive unfair or unequal treatment.

Related Literature

        Because of the quantity of publication, it is impossible
to cite every article that might be pertinent. Only repre-

sentative views will be noted; and in many instances, e.g.,
the opinions on the education of academic librarians, the
literature tends to be repetitious. That the literature is
repetitious is not of itself blameworthy. Look at the studies
on Shakespeare. Similarly, as Berelson found in examining
the history of graduate education in the United States, the
same or at least similar views on such matters as the quality of students, the place of research in graduate study, the
dissertation itself, the meaning of the master's and the doctor's degrees, and the appropriate preparation for college
teachers have appeared over and over. [7] He concluded that
the fact that the debate on these vital issues "has been un-
changing and indecisive does not necessarily imply that it
should not be taken seriously." [8]

This applies most emphatically to the present review
of the literature. Because the views on such important matters as the most desirable educational preparation of academic librarians are largely a matter of opinion, a range of
viewpoints needs to be examined. As is true of the views
on graduate education in the United States, whether a particular statement dates from 1920 or 1940 or 1970 does not of
itself make it any more nor less pertinent. It should be
noted too that the continuing discussion of the appropriate
educational requirements of academic librarians is desirable
and reflects an abiding concern for one of the central issues
of the profession.

Certain other issues such as tenure for librarians
have received comparatively little attention, although a number of important articles have appeared on the subject recently. Furthermore, in examining the questions regarding
matters such as faculty rank or research and publication, it
is essential to pay heed to the faculty point of view.

Disregarding writings on higher education has been a
pronounced weakness of many previous studies. Librarians
have ignored discussions of criteria for appointment, promotion, and tenure at their own peril. Arguing for equality of
treatment in salaries, sabbatical leaves, tenure, etc. may
in some instances reflect an ignorance of existing practices
in higher education and a demand, not for equality of treatment but for preferential treatment. In most institutions
degrees and scholarship, for example, do make a difference.

Thus, in reviewing the literature, emphasis is placed
on showing the range of opinion on topics pertinent to faculty

status, and discussions from other disciplines are cited. Part
I of this paper, then, examines various points of view and
summarizes previous surveys to establish a "climate of
opinion" for a discussion in Part II of the status of academic
librarians in the 19 institutions surveyed for the present
study.

Definitions and Limitations

For the purposes of clarity in this paper academic
status for librarians may be defined, as does ACRL, [9] as an
official recognition by the institutions that librarians are part
of the instructional and research staff. Faculty status, as
distinct from academic status, also includes faculty rank and
titles, but titles and rank alone have little meaning. To be
significant faculty status also must insure such benefits as:

1) Commensurate salary;
2) Eligibility for sabbatical leaves and leaves of
   absence;
3) Access to research grants;
4) Tenure;
5) Voting privileges in the institution's governing body;
6) Eligibility for election to faculty committees;
7) Vacations identical with those of faculty members.

While the ACRL resolution quoted above refers to important matters regarding the performance of only professional tasks, grievance procedures, participation in library
government, and peer review of appointment and promotion,
these factors would more appropriately be investigated in a
separate research project and are, therefore, excluded from
this study. These are, of course, internal matters which
librarians should be able to solve on their own, without regard to the faculty or institutional policies. If librarians as
a professional group have the necessary leadership abilities,
they should be able to make library management more democratic.

To gather data on the benefits of faculty status as outlined above a questionnaire was sent to all full-time professional librarians and a random sample of faculty members in
19 state colleges and universities in Michigan, Minnesota, and
Wisconsin. In addition, both the librarians and the faculty
were asked to assess the status of librarians in relation to
a selected group of other professional personnel on campus.
The responsibilities of faculty status such as professional

activities, participation in institutional government, education,
research, and publication were investigated.

The sample was limited to librarians and full-time
faculty members employed at the main campuses of the following 19 institutions of higher learning:

Michigan: Central Michigan University, Eastern Michigan University, Northern Michigan University, and
Western Michigan University.

Minnesota: Bemidji State College, Mankato State College, Moorhead State College, Saint Cloud State College, Southwest Minnesota State College, and Winona
State College.

Wisconsin: Wisconsin State University at Eau Claire,
Wisconsin State University at La Crosse, Wisconsin
State University at Oshkosh, Wisconsin State Univer-
sity at Platteville, Wisconsin State University at River
Falls, Wisconsin State University at Stevens Point,
Wisconsin State University at Superior, Wisconsin State
University at Whitewater, and Stout State University.

As a group, these 19 institutions are similar to many state
colleges and universities in other parts of the country. Although they are involved mainly with undergraduate education,
most of them offer some graduate work at the master's level,
and a few are already engaged in or are developing doctoral
programs. Enrollments for the 1969 spring term ranged
from about 2,000 to 20,000. [10]

As stated above, the study included all full-time professional librarians employed in the 19 institutions. The determination of who is a professional librarian was left to the
head librarian of each institution. Thus "librarian" is defined on the operational level; that is, all those librarians
who were considered members of the professional staff by
the head librarians were included in the survey. Because
the status of librarians is decided on the local level and because the qualifications and achievements of the library staff
at a particular institution to a considerable extent determine
their acceptance by the faculty, this seemed the most appropriate procedure.

To provide a basis for comparison with the librarians,
questionnaires were sent to a random sample of full-time

faculty members from the departments of history, English,
sociology, economics, physics, and biology.

For the purposes of analysis the older fifth-year bachelor's degree in library science is considered the equivalent
of the present fifth-year master's degree. Similarly, the
older sixth-year master's degree is considered the equivalent
of the present sixth-year certificate in library science.

Methodology

Part I of the study reviews the literature and summarizes surveys on the faculty and academic status of librarians. This section includes discussions both of the benefits
and the responsibilities of faculty status.

To gather information on current conditions, a questionnaire was sent to all the professional librarians in the 19
state colleges and universities selected for the study. A
second questionnaire was sent to a random sample of full-
time faculty members in the same institutions. The questionnaires were pre-tested on a group of 20 graduate students
at the University of Michigan. The results of the survey are
analyzed in Part II.

In some instances slight discrepancies may exist in
the tabulated information due to the necessity to round off
numbers beyond the decimal point. The Mann-Whitney U-test
for differences between independent samples and chi-square
were applied selectively to determine the statistical significance of the findings.

Questions Investigated

The questionnaires were designed to investigate current conditions relating to both responsibilities and benefits
of faculty status. In addition to information on characteristics such as age, sex, and experience the survey instrument
sought answers to the following questions:

1) Do librarians and faculty members have comparable
education and comparable educational goals?

2) Are faculty members and librarians under the same
pressure to work toward the doctorate?

3) To become head librarian, does a librarian need

a level of education and scholarship comparable to that required for a faculty member to become a full professor?

4) To what extent do librarians and faculty members engage in research and writing?

5) Do librarians and faculty members devote a comparable amount of time to professional activities?

6) Do librarians and faculty members devote a comparable amount of time to service on academic committees?

7) Do librarians and faculty members have voting privileges in the institution's governing body on a comparable basis?

8) Are salaries for librarians comparable to those for faculty members with similar educational background and experience?

9) Is the salary range for librarians comparable to that for faculty members?

10) Do librarians and faculty members have comparable opportunity for sabbatical leaves?

11) Are librarians and faculty members eligible for tenure on a comparable basis?

12) Do librarians and faculty members have comparable vacations?

13) Do librarians and faculty members have access to research grants and travel funds on a comparable basis?

14) How do librarians rank in comparison with other professional positions?

In summary, these are the major issues which seem pertinent when examining the question of faculty status for college and university librarians, for both the benefits and the responsibilities of faculty status must be considered before one can draw conclusions as to whether librarians receive equitable treatment.

Notes

1. "Atlantic City Conference: A Great Show in Two Parts
    and a Cast of Thousands, " ALA Bulletin, 63 (July-
    August, 1969), 925-26.

2. Ibid., pp. 952-53.

3. Ibid., pp. 945-47

4. Ibid., p. 953.

5. "Status of Academic Librarians in California, " California
    Librarian, 29 (January, 1968), 37-38.

6. Ibid., pp. 38-39.

7. Bernard Berelson, Graduate Education in the United
    States (New York: McGraw-Hill Book Company, Inc.,
    1960), pp. 6-42.

8. Ibid., p. 41.

9. "Status of College and University Librarians, " College
    and Research Libraries, 20 (September, 1959), 400.

10. World Almanac and Book of Facts (1970 ed.; New York:
    Newspaper Enterprise Association, Inc., 1969), pp.
    318-32. Southwest Minnesota State College is the
    smallest institution. Since it is a new college which
    opened in 1967, enrollment figures are not in the
    World Almanac but were obtained from the institution
    itself.

PART I

RELATED LITERATURE

Chapter 2

The Question of Faculty or Academic Status

Definitions of Academic and Faculty Status

In spite of the voluminous discussions of the question
there is still no accepted definition of academic or faculty
status, and the two terms have often been used interchangeably.   To an outsider looking at the matter dispassionately,
this might well come as a surprise, for it is rather unusual
for a professional group to argue for something without first
defining precisely what it wants.

Forgotson defined status as the relative position an
individual occupies within an organization or a social group.
Since it carries with it certain rights and duties with regard
to a particular role to be performed, status also represents
the value and rewards accorded to that position. [1] If society
deems certain tasks important, it will, according to Barber,
attribute esteem to the individuals performing those tasks.
Because of their contribution to society, physicians enjoy
more prestige than either lawyers or bankers, and the two
latter groups are more highly esteemed than bookkeepers,
carpenters, or bartenders.   Also, individuals within a group
may rank higher or lower than the entire group.   Thus the
accomplished lawyer enjoys more prestige than one who
handles only minor legal matters, a skilled surgeon more
than a general practitioner. [2]

Although it is not the purpose of this study to examine
the characteristics of professions, it is worth noting the major determinants of occupational prestige.   In his study of
the rise of the professions in nineteenth century England,
Reader showed that education

came to be regarded as important in judging professional
standing generally.   From the point of view of the socially ambitious, the great virtue of education was that
it could be acquired, whereas a string of ancestors could
not. [3]

11

According to the Barber study, both among professional and other

> functionally important social roles, the greater the
> amount of systematic and generalized knowledge, the
> higher the evaluation and the consequent stratificational
> position. [4]

As far as the individual is concerned, responsibility is also a factor.

> The greater the amount of knowledge or responsibility,
> or the two in combination, required for performance in
> a given role, the higher the stratificational position of
> the incumbent of that position. [5]

Conversely, those occupations which have low esteem entail little knowledge or responsibility. The knowledge itself must be systematic and generalized, not just long training in manual dexterity as for an athlete, for example. By responsibility Barber means the number of people an individual "controls" either directly or indirectly. [6] When applied to libraries, this would mean that the director of a large library may be regarded more highly than the director of a small one because the former "controls" more employees. Ben-David holds that there is no universally accepted nor unequivocal definition of professions, only a set of characteristics which are present in different degrees in various occupations. But higher education is the most important element in professionalism. [7]

Status, then, has implications both for the individual and for the group. It represents the relative position an individual holds within an organization or a profession, or in society. The profession itself is also accorded a relative position in the prestige structure.

The literature contains a number of definitions of academic or faculty status. Commenting on the librarian's position in colleges and universities, Hintz indicated in 1968 that the "exact definition of academic status remains uncertain."[8] On the practical level the lack of precise terminology is evident from the surveys both before and after 1968. Writers have sometimes used faculty status and academic status interchangeably or have used one or the other without stating what they meant by their terms.

In 1927 Works felt that the most significant compo-

nents of the librarian's status were "salary, retirement pro-
visions, length of vacations, tenure, relationship to faculty,
and conditions governing attendance at professional meetings."[9]
In 1941 Randall and Goodrich stressed the point that the
status of the librarian could be better discerned from the
conditions of employment than from statements of administrative officials. [10]

Hoping to improve their status, the College Library
Division of the Texas Library Association, on April 15, 1950,
unanimously endorsed a proposal which sought rank and titles
based on educational background and experience, salaries
equivalent to faculty members with adjustments for longer
terms of service, and

> rights and privileges equivalent to those of classroom
> teachers in regard to holiday and vacation periods
> within the academic year, inclusion in college social
> affairs, sick leave, group insurance, retirement bene-
> fits, attendance at faculty meetings, service on faculty
> committees and tenure of position. [11]

McAnally's definition dating from 1957 is representative of the working assumptions often used by the surveyors. He drew distinctions but failed to apply them.

> Faculty status for librarians is defined as the posses-
> sion of all or most of the privileges of the classroom
> teaching faculty, including faculty rank. Academic
> status is held to be the possession of some but not all
> usual faculty privileges, with definite classification as
> academic but always without faculty rank. Academic
> status thus may be considered a kind of reduced fac-
> ulty status. Because faculty status and academic
> status are quite similar, and for convenience, the term
> academic status is used loosely throughout the rest of
> this paper to apply to both forms. [12]

Expressing a concern about the problem but without resolv-
ing the quandary, Downs in 1957 commented on the lack of
precision in terminology:

> A number of librarians with whom I correspond made
> the point that we need a definition of academic status.
> Is it, for example, identical with faculty status? Here
> is evidently a question of semantics requiring clarifi-
> cation; otherwise, we will often be talking at cross

purposes. In many universities, academic status and
faculty rank are not considered the same thing. The
librarian may feel that he has achieved academic status
if he and his staff have been granted certain faculty
perquisites, such as attending faculty meetings and
marching in academic processions, even though these
are not accompanied by academic titles. It is obvious
that under this interpretation academic status is something less than full faculty standing. [13]

Wilson and Tauber in 1956 neatly evaded the dilemma by re-
ferring to "faculty academic status."[14]

In 1959 the Committee on Academic Status of the
University Libraries Section of ACRL also, and apparently
deliberately, evaded the question of differences between faculty and academic status by ignoring the former and defining
only the latter:

Academic status for professional librarians may be defined as the formal recognition, in writing, by an institution's authorities, of librarians as members of the
instructional and research staff. The recognition may
take the form of assigned faculty ranks and titles, or
equivalent ranks and titles, according to institutional
custom. [15]

Not until 1968 did a survey begin with a precise
working definition when Madan, Hetler, and Strong wrote that
"full faculty status"

entails complete equality with the academic faculty in
regard to rank and titles, promotion criteria, tenure,
sabbatical leave, rates of pay, holidays and vacations,
representation and participation in faculty government
and fringe benefits. [16]

In addition to the points in the above definition the ACRL resolution of 1969 stipulates that librarians must be responsible
only for professional tasks, be appointed and promoted on the
basis of individual accomplishment and peer review, have
access to research funds, participate in library government,
and have grievance and appeal procedures involving peer review. [17]

Previous Surveys of Academic and Faculty Status
in State Colleges and Universities

The review of previous surveys will be restricted to
those studies which examined conditions in state colleges and
universities and which encompassed more than one institution
and more than one state.

Because terminology has not always been used with
precision in the past, it is sometimes difficult to interpret
the results of the previous surveys. Nevertheless, it is
possible to arrive at general definitions which apply in most
instances. Academic status has ordinarily meant that librarians are members of the instructional and research staff.
Generally, faculty status has meant that the librarian had an
academic rank and title without regard to benefits. Especially in recent years, some librarians have begun to insist
that they have "full faculty status" only if this includes all of
the factors cited in the 1969 ACRL resolution.

As early as 1941, Estes reported a growing trend
toward faculty status for librarians. [18] By 1956 Wilson and
Tauber reported a definite trend toward "faculty academic
status, " as they called it, during the previous decade for
those who merited it by virtue of their education and responsibility; but they found no uniformity of practice in matters of tenure, salaries, time for research and study, vacations, or travel. [19] Somewhat more cautiously, Lyle wrote
in 1961 that a definite though gradual trend toward academic
status was noticeable in American colleges. However, while
librarians enjoyed many of the faculty rights and privileges,
few librarians, regardless of their status, received salaries,
vacations, and sabbaticals equal to faculty members. [20]

The Committee on Academic Status of the University
Libraries Section of ACRL stated in 1959 that over half of the
colleges and universities in the United States had given academic status to the professional members of the library
staff. [21] Downs found "solid, if perhaps unspectacular, progress" from 1957 to 1964. [22] Similar statements can be
found in other books and articles. In spite of the apparent
optimism exhibited by most of those writers, Madan, Hetler,
and Strong recently interjected a more gloomy note. Using
a definition of status which included both faculty rank and
benefits, they found that only 14. 2% of the respondents had
full faculty status. [23] Nevertheless, regardless of the apparent contradictions, much progress has been made as an ex-

amination of a number of surveys in chronological order will
demonstrate.

Table 1 shows the percentage of librarians with faculty or academic status as reported in various surveys of
academic libraries in the United States.   Apparently the first
survey of the status of academic librarians was that by Henry
in 1911.   Focusing on 17 institutions, of which 16 replied,
his study may serve as some indication of existing conditions.
He found that the chief librarian usually had the rank of professor.   In those institutions which had an assistant or associate librarian (used here to designate a high administrative
position immediately below the director), that person often
also had academic rank, but faculty rank for librarians was
usually restricted to the highest or the two highest positions.
In only one institution did all librarians have academic rank.[24]

Using a sample of 18 institutions, Works wrote in
1927 that in all but two cases the chief librarian held the
rank of professor.   Institutions which had an assistant or
associate librarian also usually accorded faculty status to
those individuals.   Evidence of some progress from 1911 to
1927 is shown by the fact that a few institutions had extended
faculty rank to certain individuals below the position of chief
and associate librarian or, in a few instances, to all members of the staff.   However, no exact figures were reported,
and in most cases the staff was either uncertain of its status
or relegated to a clerical level. [25]

Klein reported in 1930 that in 48 land-grant colleges
and universities 23 head librarians held the rank of professor,
four were associate professors, five were assistant professors, and one was an instructor.   Furthermore, nine library
department heads held the rank of instructor or assistant
professor. [26]   The next study, chronologically, was by Maloy.
An explanation of her survey presents problems, for she
stated that the findings

> should be used with some caution, however, as the per-
> centage of nonfaculty librarians who asked that their
> reports be held confidential was more than 1 1/2 times
> the percentage of faculty librarians making the same
> request. [27]

Exactly what this means is not clear.   Did she exclude those
which asked that their replies be kept confidential?   Also,
how did she select her sample and what percentage responded?

And what, by her standards, is a large college or university and what is a small college? Then there is also the problem of definitions:

> When a librarian says 'academic rank not specified, ' is he saying diplomatically that he has no faculty privileges? or does he mean that such good feeling exists in his institution that there is no discrimination against the librarians and that the issue has never formally been raised?[28]

In spite of these difficulties her study is of interest because it apparently included a national sample of 129 libraries, and it examined conditions in large colleges and universities, small colleges, and teachers' colleges.

In summary, Maloy reported in 1939 that of 129 chief librarians, 98 had faculty status (but of these 18 had nominal status), and 31 did not have faculty status. Among the associate librarians 30 had faculty status (seven had nominal status) and 40 did not have faculty status. Twenty-seven department heads had faculty status; of these four had nominal status; and 23 had no faculty status. All librarians had faculty status in 20 institutions, and in 30 they did not. While differences between the teachers colleges, small colleges, and large colleges and universities were small, the small colleges appeared to be somewhat more reluctant to grant faculty status to librarians than other types of institutions. [29]

With but one or two exceptions, the surveys since Maloy tended to deal with only one type of library or with a limited geographical region. McMillen, in his study of 37 large university libraries with holdings of over 200, 000 volumes, stated that the director usually had the rank of professor, with one or two listed as dean. Although not all libraries had such positions, the associate librarians had faculty rank in 20 institutions, but in only 11 cases were department heads classified with the faculty. [30] Restricting his investigation in 1948 to 70 liberal arts colleges, teachers colleges and small universities in the East, Gelfand found that 24% of the 50 reporting institutions granted faculty status to all librarians whereas 72% of the head librarians had faculty rank. [31]

Spain's results showed that all librarians had faculty status in 62% of 108 southern colleges and universities, in

TABLE 1

Selected Previous Surveys on the Academic
or Faculty Status of Librarians

Identification (date, author, inclusion)	Proportion of Librarians with Academic or Faculty Status	
	Head Librarian	Professional Staff
1911. Henry. 16 institutions in various parts of the country	Usually	All had rank in 1; in 15 few or none had it
1927. Works. 18 major libraries	89%	Most librarians classified as clerical or uncertain
1930. Klein. 48 land-grant institutions	69%	*
1939. Maloy. 129 libraries all parts of U.S., all types of institutions	76%	40%
1940. McMillen. 37 large universities	Usually	*
1948. Gelfand. 50 replies from liberal arts colleges, teachers colleges, and small universities in the East	72%	24%
1948. Spain. 108 southern colleges and universities	92%	All librarians in 62%; 1 or a few in 31%; none in 8%
1950. Schick. Head librarians in 155 large colleges and universities	94%	
1950. Stieg. 23% return from 1,695 colleges, universities, teachers colleges, technical schools, and junior colleges; about 399 returns	*	55%, i.e., over half of professional staff had faculty status

Identification (date, author, inclusion)	Proportion of Librarians with Academic or Faculty Status	
	Head Librarian	Professional Staff
1951. Lundy. 36 colleges and universities	*	39% faculty status; 22% academic status
1953. Muller. 49 medium sized universities	86%	39% faculty status
1957. McAnally. 97 colleges and universities	*	31% academic status; 25% faculty status
1957. Downs. 115 leading universities	*	30% faculty status; 23% academic status
1964. Downs. State universities	*	From 1957 solid progress--faculty or academic status in several more institutions
1968. Hintz. 87 large colleges and universities	*	80% academic status of some kind; 30% faculty status
1968. Madan, Hetler, and Strong. 183, 4-year state colleges and universities	*	14. 2% full faculty status; 63. 4% said they had it
1970. Cassata. 57 members of Association of Research Libraries	*	40% academic status; 30. 9% faculty status

*Figures not given or data incomplete.

31% only the head librarians or a few others had it, and in
8% of the cases no member of the staff had it. [32]   From this
it would seem that librarians in the South were more likely
to have faculty status than were librarians in other parts of
the country at that time.   However, even for those librarians
who had faculty status, she found many differences between
faculty members and librarians in salaries, vacations, tenure,
and participation in faculty government.

　　　　　While primarily concerned with retirement plans for
academic librarians, Stieg in 1950 included statistics showing
that 55% of the professional staff had faculty status.   Results
in this case were based on a 23% return from 1,695 colleges,
universities, teachers colleges, professional and technical
schools, and junior colleges throughout the United States.
Only librarians in those institutions surveyed which assigned
faculty status to over half of the professional staff were
counted as having faculty status. [33]   Schick wrote in 1950 that
94% of the 155 respondents had faculty status, but his study
was limited to head librarians in large colleges and universities. [34]   The following year Lundy described conditions in
36 colleges and universities.   The entire staff had faculty
status in 14, in eight more they were classified with the faculty in some fashion, in seven the librarians were attempting
to resolve the question, and in seven they did not consider it
appropriate. [35]

　　　　　Examining conditions in 49 medium-sized colleges
and universities in 1953, Muller found that in 19 institutions
the entire professional staff had faculty rank, in 28 some in
addition to the head librarian had rank, in 14 only the head
librarian had rank, and in seven none had it. [36]   McAnally in
his 1957 survey of 97 colleges and universities reported that
librarians had academic status in 30 institutions and in 24
they had faculty status. [37]   In the same year Downs found that
in 35 of 115 leading American universities librarians had
faculty status and titles, while in 27 they had academic
status. [38]   In a follow-up study, Downs in 1964 reported
"solid, if perhaps unspectacular, progress" since 1957 with
librarians in a number of state universities having gained
faculty or academic status, but few changes had occurred in
private institutions. [39]

　　　　　Hintz had difficulty in categorizing the array of divergent practices in his 87 replies from questionnaires sent
to 71 members of the Association of Research Libraries and
29 other institutions, most of which were state universities.

In 70 of the 87, librarians had academic status of some kind but only 26 had faculty rank and titles, 13 had equivalent rank, seven had assimilated rank, and 24 he classified as a variable group because conditions could not readily be categorized. [40]

The only survey which used an explicit definition of what constitutes faculty status was that by Madan, Hetler, and Strong.   They maintained that unless librarians received equal treatment with faculty members in matters of salaries, sabbaticals, vacations, rank and title, tenure, promotion criteria, fringe benefits, and participation in institutional government, they did not have faculty status.   On this basis, librarians in 26 (14.2%) of 183 state colleges and universities had faculty status whereas 63.4% said they had it. [41]   Just two years later, Cassata reported that among 57 members of the Association of Research Libraries 40% had academic status and 30.9% had faculty status, [42] but the increase over the Madan, Hetler, and Strong survey probably resulted from a difference in the application of terminology.

Thus it seems that the majority of librarians have gained acceptance in the academic community.   From 1911 to 1970 the increase is especially noticeable at the lower levels.   Among the top administrative group a rather high percentage have been classified with the faculty for many years, but in more and more cases the entire professional staff is gaining acceptance.   However, it must be emphasized that in many instances the recognition of librarians has meant only that they are increasingly being designated as academic staff rather than being classified as administrative personnel or in some other way.   As far as "full faculty status" is concerned, the percentages still seem to be rather low.

What Kind of Status Do Librarians Want?

More than 20 years ago Gelfand found divergent opinions among head librarians as to whether the staff should be classified as administrative or instructional. [43]   While Downs in 1957 reported that most university librarians agreed that close identification with the faculty was essential, the chief administrators suggested the following as possible solutions to the problem: (1) full faculty status including suitable rank and titles;   (2) using a system of academic classification and assigning equivalent rank;   (3) defining librarians as academic but without explicit identification with faculty ranks;

or (4) "other means." Those identifying with the latter group
usually favored an independent, self-reliant position for librarians. Some hoped the profession might ultimately win
recognition as a distinct and honored profession. Because
they maintained that each institution has its own peculiarities
and problems, some library administrators believed that no
single, uniform solution was appropriate to all. [44]

Usually academic status is easier to achieve than faculty status, [45] but that of itself is no reason for seeking one
in preference to the other. Along the lines of deliberate
separation, Klein in 1930 went so far as to say that the title
"librarian" should be more important than that of "professor."[46] To affirm that librarians should remain separate by
choice and should work toward achieving prestige as librarians rather than "inherit" their status by association with the
faculty is, of course, different from stoic resignation to the
existing situation and refraining from any efforts to alter it.
Along these lines, Downs in 1957 surveyed the views of directors of large university libraries in the United States.
Raynard Swank suggested that the entire university staff
should be divided into two groups, academic and non-aca-
demic. The academic would be divided into two groups, one
including teachers and the other including librarians, research
personnel, counselors, etc. This would avoid the difficulty
of fitting librarians into categories defined for teaching.
Swank preferred to see librarians recognized as academic but
separate from the faculty, not "'dependent for their status
upon the imitation of faculty ranks.'" Robert Vosper insisted
that librarians could achieve whatever status they desired if
they proved themselves worthy contributors to scholarship by
publication and full participation in academic affairs. Similarly, Paul Buck believed that librarians should stand on their
own feet as contributors to the institution's educational endeavors. When they make an acceptable contribution, librarians should have the same benefits as the faculty. Expressing similar views were Guy Lyle, Eugene Wilson, Benjamin
Powell, and John Berthel. Lewis Stieg, William Ready,
Marvin Miller, and William Dix spoke for equivalent classification schedules not tied directly to the academic ranks of
the teaching faculty. Donald Coney and Lawrence Powell
considered civil service satisfactory in the University of California system. [47]

Because the surveys by Downs and Gelfand were based
on replies from head librarians, they provide no means of
judging the opinions of professional librarians in general.

Unfortunately Schiller's recent report does not include exact
figures, but she does say that few of the 2,282 respondents
in her survey dissented from the principle of faculty status.[48]
Whether this reflects a change caused by time or a difference
of opinion between chief librarians and other professionals
cannot be determined. Investigating attitudes of librarians
and faculty members in public junior colleges in Michigan,
Meyer in 1968 found that 63% of the head librarians thought
that librarians should be classified as administrators or in
some other fashion, not with the faculty. Among librarians
other than the director, 30.2% held the same opinion, as did
46.4% of the faculty. [49]

Reasons for Seeking Faculty Status

        Motivations for seeking faculty status, although inter-
related, may be summarized under three broad headings.
(1) Some librarians seek an improved status as an end in itself and for social reasons. They want the academic community to accord more prestige to librarians. At the same
time they may wish to be more readily accepted on a social
level. (2) Another reason for seeking faculty status is that
acceptance by the faculty as peers in the educational enterprise increases the librarians' opportunity to be of service.
(3) Finally, some librarians seek faculty status primarily for
the sake of the concomitant benefits.

        Status for Its Own Sake and Social Status. --That li-
brarians in general and academic librarians in particular have
long been concerned about their status is no secret, [50] and
librarians have been accused of seeking faculty rank almost
as an end in itself. [51] Writing in 1963, Lyle felt that placing
less emphasis on status would help library-administrative relations. [52] Generally the abiding concern for faculty status
has been more of a local and personal struggle than an effort
by librarians as a group. This would seem to be supported
by Naegele and Stolar who concluded, on the basis of their
1960 study in the Pacific Northwest, that librarians were
more concerned about being individually good librarians and
gaining personal prestige than in launching a crusade on be-
half of the profession. [53]

        To McEwen the librarian's quest for faculty status in-
volves a desire for recognition and acceptance by the academic community. On a purely personal level this might
mean invitations to dinner parties or participation in bridge

clubs.   At a large university McEwen felt social acceptance
was less of an issue, for librarians could fraternize with each
other.   However, in a small college social acceptance was an
important factor.   Nevertheless, formal status can bear fruit
only when actual status is given by those who can give it, the
faculty.   Real acceptance must, of course, also be won by
the individual. [54]

Although not an end in themselves, social standing, informal contacts, and friendship, Branscomb wrote, were more
important than official connections. [55]   Forgotson feared that
librarians were not accepted socially on the same basis as
other professionals.   Even when the librarian's official status
is clear, his actual status may still be ambiguous because
students and the faculty may regard him as a super clerk or
administrative aide.   In psychological terms Forgotson viewed
this as an unhealthy condition.   Because the librarian does
not have a clear sense of identity, he is not integrated into
the academic community and cannot function at an optimal
level. [56]

Some of the uneasiness of librarians regarding their
status may stem from the way in which this problem has been
treated in library literature.   Imbued with a desire to be of
service and convinced that the library is essential to the institution's educational objectives, librarians may feel frus-
trated because they are not as effective as they think they
ought to be.   According to Guinagh, librarians feel physically
and psychologically isolated.   They want to be appreciated
but feel thwarted because the faculty and administration do
not place as much value on their contribution as do librarians
themselves.   And this, he maintains, is not the baseless re-
action of a few oversensitive souls. [57]   Similarly, the recent
study by Heim and Cameron suggests that their present treatment may reflect a low evaluation of librarians' contribution
to the educational process. [58]

Possibly some librarians feel insecure or inadequate
if they have not achieved a level of recognition deemed appropriate by their peers.   In 1932 Randall stated, "The importance assigned by the college administrator to the library may
usually be inferred from the qualifications of the library
staff. "[59]   Downs has made the same point in greater detail
a number of times:

Just as we can judge the college or university in terms
of its library, so we can judge the library in terms of

its staff. If the librarians are recognized as an integral part of the academic ranks, if they are a vital
group in the educational process, with high qualifications for appointment, and all the rights and privileges
of other academic employees, we can feel confident that
library will rank high in all-round effectiveness. On
the other hand, if the professional library personnel are
in some nondescript category, without clearly defined
status, with no institutional understanding of the contributions which they can make to the educational program,
and if they are placed outside, or made ineligible for,
the usual academic perquisites and prerogatives,
we can be equally certain that the library is inferior,
falling far below its best potentialities. There is a
difference. The institution can pay its money and take
its choice. [60]

From this the reader could infer that the librarian who does not
have faculty status is somehow inferior, for having faculty
status is a measure of whether the librarian has met "high
qualifications for appointment. "

If what Knapp says is accurate, faculty members
themselves are status conscious, for she maintains that academic rank is a status symbol which may be jealously guard-
ed against all intruders. If he is admitted to the ranks, the
librarian is accepted because he has gained respect as a
scholar, an educator, or a bookman. [61]

A number of recent studies would seem to support
Knapp's assertion. Three recent doctoral dissertations have
dealt with the image of the professor in popular periodicals. [62] Other dissertations have been done on the status of
teachers in schools of education[63] and on the prestige of
members of the instructional staff in a university. [64]

As far as prestige in American society is concerned,
academic librarians would stand to gain by close identification with the faculty. A survey of 90 occupations in 1947,
repeated in 1963, showed some changes, but in both instances
college professors ranked eighth. In 1963 they were ranked
on the same level as members of the U. S. Cabinet and re-
presentatives in Congress, below justices of the Supreme
Court, physicians, state governors, and nuclear physicists
but above lawyers, dentists, U. S. diplomats, architects,
ministers, priests, bankers, novelists, musicians, and so on.
Unfortunately librarians were not included in the list, but it

seems likely that they would have been well below the number eight position. [65]

Status as a Means to Providing the Opportunity for
Better Service--A second argument for close identification
between librarians and faculty members is that it enhances
the librarian's ability to render quality service. On the
grounds of the commonly accepted criterion that a profession
is altruistic, one could contend that the most cogent basis
for a discussion of faculty status for librarians is their contribution to educational objectives. But some writers ask
whether librarians have the necessary educational background
and scholarly outlook to be capable of giving the level of
service needed. Consequently, this aspect of status may
generate conflict.

Bundy and Wasserman in 1968 asserted that American
librarianship, in spite of its shortcomings, has a proud tra-
dition of service. [66] As long ago as 1880 Winsor talked about
the librarian as a teacher of teachers. The librarian, both
by direct and indirect means, can bring books to the attention of faculty members; and this is a significant way of
keeping the professor informed, which is an educational activity of high order. [67] Even earlier, from the time of the
American Library Association, prominent writers such as
Melvil Dewey stressed the educational potential of libraries
and librarians. "The time is when a library is a school,
and the librarian is in the highest sense a teacher, and the
visitor is a reader among the books as a workmen among his
tools. "[68] Furthermore, because he deals with books, reviews, announcements, etc. as part of his daily task, the librarian should be better informed about book production than
the faculty and can recommend works in their fields of interest. Thus, in addition to contributing to the building of a
worthwhile collection, the librarian can maintain close, personal contacts with faculty members which will tend to create
a working relationship of mutual respect and confidence. [69]
Robert Haro found a relationship between faculty status and
the librarians' participation in book selection; that is, in
those institutions in which librarians were active participants
in book selection they were more likely to have faculty status;
whereas the opposite was the case when faculty members had
virtually total responsibility for building the collection.

It is interesting to note that of the libraries that do not
engage in book selection, four out of the five have
neither academic nor faculty status for their librarians.[70]

The reference librarian is the most regular and conspicuous participant in education, both through teaching the
student how to use the library and in recommending particular sources for consultation. Nevertheless, administrative or
management aspects of library operations are only means to
the end of participation in the educational objectives of the
college or university. Wilson and Tauber in 1956 made this
point when they discussed the administration of the library on
"a teaching and research, as contrasted with a library-house-
keeping level. "[71] Both Wilson and Tauber[72] and Lyle[73] examined this concept at considerable length and cited other
discussions of the idea. To many academic librarians, then,
faculty status is a just reward for their contribution and a
recognition of their educational responsibilities. Without it
the opportunity for service is greatly diminished.

If the library is deemed an essential part of education
and research, McAnally wrote in 1957, the battle is half won;
and to a considerable extent the quality of service will determine the prestige of the library. Whether the head librarian is accepted by the faculty is critical, but the library
staff itself must be alert and contribute in individual teaching
and research. At the same time, lack of the doctorate is a
hurdle, and too many librarians do not want to be measured
by faculty standards such as degrees, research, and publications. [74]

Academic status requires professionalism in the real
sense of the word rather than the watered-down version
commonly used. Too many librarians do not want to be
academicians, at least are unwilling to pay the price, to
submit to the same rigid standards of judgment which
teaching faculty members apply to themselves and their
colleagues. If full faculty status is to be requested, librarians must make clear that they are willing to accept
faculty responsibilities for membership in committees,
participation in the intellectual life of the institution, and
research and publication. [75]

Regardless of the quality of service or of the library
staff, problems may still exist. Since the professor enjoys
his role as teacher and since the book can to some extent at
least replace him, the book itself, as Marchant suggested in
1969, may represent a potential threat. On the other hand,
the concept of self-education augments the librarian's role,
and he takes every opportunity to attract readers. The first
important conflict, then, between librarians and the faculty

developed out of the librarian's desire to encourage greater
use of the collection. [76]

Blackburn in 1968 also discussed possible areas of
conflict such as the ownership of books, influence with students, the predominance of women on the library staff, status,
and roles.   Although the librarian may in certain instances
know more about books and what students should read, the
faculty member has a greater opportunity to guide students.
This may create a feeling of jealousy with the librarian who,
when the occasion presents itself, can show his superiority
by assisting the faculty member in finding information. [77]

Although Scherer in 1960 concluded that library-faculty
relationships in liberal arts colleges were satisfactory, his
results indicate potential areas of disharmony.   To cite but a
few examples regarding the availability and use of books, 28%
of the faculty felt that some important books were not available, and 22% of the librarians felt that faculty members
failed to order books on time.   While 91% of the librarians
stated that books could be used before they were cataloged,
77% of the faculty thought this was possible.   Among the librarians 67% thought reading lists for classes were revised
regularly and 87% of the faculty said they were not. [78] Should
any of these matters become an issue, the library staff may
encounter opposition when seeking faculty status.   As
McAnally stated in 1957, a small minority of vocal faculty
members can block an attempt to gain faculty status for librarians. [79]

Monteith College was designed to foster independent
learning.   In order to achieve the desired objectives, instruction in library use had to be closely related to course
instruction and content, said Knapp in 1966.   Since a knowledge of how to use the library effectively is essential to lifelong learning, the educator should include this competence as
one of the major objectives of a liberal or general education.
In the Monteith project librarians had to learn a great deal
about course planning, what students should do, how material
should be presented, how to evaluate the work of students,
etc.   Even under what might be considered ideal conditions,
librarians were not completely accepted by some of the faculty members, and some of the faculty members lacked the
necessary knowledge to exploit the resources of the library
fully. [80]

According to Guinagh, writing in 1963, the most

vociferous objections to faculty status for librarians may
come from those faculty members who seldom use the library. [81]   Others, because they may not understand the problems, may look upon library records and administrative matters as simple, repetitive, "mechanical details. "[82]   In response to those who would maintain that librarians should be
in a unique classification, McAnally thought in 1957 that a
separate classification posed problems on the practical level
because librarians are a small group with limited influence
and can therefore easily become isolated and lose their
effectiveness. [83]

Carlson in 1955 saw an historical basis for the faculty
member's low esteem for librarians.   In the early stages of
the development of academic libraries in the United States the
librarian personally handled all the details from writing the
order for the books to paying the bills, stamping the date due
slip, and making sure that the book was returned on time.
Carlson thought that part of this image still persisted. [84]   If
this is indeed the case, it would appear that some faculty
members believe librarians to be incapable of rendering an
educational service.   But Lundy in 1951 asserted that the library is concerned directly with teaching and learning, with
the storage of knowledge not for its own sake but for use.   It
is imperative, therefore, that librarians have a thorough
grounding in the problems students and teachers encounter.
A sound understanding of the objectives of the institution, of
the materials required to support the curriculum, of library
procedures which are designed to support the instructional
program, demands qualifications as exacting as those required for teaching.

Many writers have affirmed, and Lundy serves as a
good example, that librarians, to perform their tasks well,
need close contact with both students and faculty members.
They need to be aware of curriculum changes, course objectives, current topics of discussion, the general cultural and
intellectual thrust of the institution.   Unless librarians attend
faculty meetings, serve on faculty committees, participate
actively in academic affairs, unless they are an integral part
of campus life, they will be less able to serve the academy.
While faculty status is not an end in itself, it provides a
means of enabling the librarians to keep in tune with the objectives of the institution they serve. [85]

Writing in 1966, David Weber submitted that librarians, because about half of them may be supervisors or

managers, have some characteristics similar to those of administrative officers, but they also share some responsibilities which are akin to those of the professor.   Thus librarians, working in a service organization, gear their energies
and activities toward the scholarly and instructional needs of
others. [86] When separated from the faculty, the librarian is
less able to serve the educational needs of the institution in
an effective way.   Therefore Marchant felt that one of the
most significant arguments for granting faculty status to librarians is that it enlarges opportunities for communication.[87]

As Branscomb wrote 30 years ago, the title of instructor or professor is not important.   But the appropriate
position within the organization is, for this may engender
cooperation and open avenues of communication.   If any educational responsibility is expected of them, it seems evident
that librarians must be classified as faculty. [88]

> If the library is to function intelligently as part of the
> educational program, the librarian must be placed in a
> position in which he will be informed as to what is
> going on.   In practical terms this means in most insti-
> tutions changing the status of the librarian.   In a great
> many colleges and universities they are not even mem-
> bers of the faculty, whose educational objectives they
> are expected to carry out. [89]

In the same vein, Bousfield in 1948 thought that the
relationship between the librarian and the faculty was so
fundamental that it was no exaggeration to link the effectiveness of the librarian with the quality of that relationship. To
develop the ideal relationship naturally takes time, but it is
essential. [90]   Similarly, Smith and Baxter in 1965 believed
that unless the librarian was formally classified as academic
he would probably fail to recognize the essentially educational
nature of his work.   Winning the respect and cooperation of
the students and faculty members would then be impossible.[91]

If the library is an integral part of the instructional
program, it follows logically, in Gelfand's view, that those
who build and organize the collection should also be classified with the instructional staff.   Excluding librarians would
seem to be an admission that the librarian, and by extension
the library, has no impact on the college program.   Similarly, if one accepts the statement that the library comple-
ments and supplements the activity of the teacher in the
classroom, it should then follow automatically that those who

are responsible for the operation of the library are also engaged in an educational enterprise. They provide personal
services, guidance, counsel, and instruction to both students
and faculty members. As for the question of the librarian
as an administrator, he says that effective administration is
a goal primarily because this will permit the library to
achieve educational objectives. [92] "Librarians generally regard the management of a library as administrative but the
function of the work performed as instructional. "[93]

Faculty Status as a Means of Gaining Faculty Benefits. --That faculty status is desirable because of the potential
benefits in salaries, vacation, tenure, retirement, etc. has
been mentioned many times. If librarians were to be candid,
Ditzion felt in 1947, they would admit that a major goal of
faculty status for librarians was to obtain salaries and other
benefits equivalent to those of the teaching staff. [94] Works
in 1927 stressed the importance of adequate compensation[95]
as did some of the respondents in Muller's survey in 1953.[96]

Other writers have also stressed the need for librarians to improve their qualifications in order to merit higher
remuneration; for contributions and rewards cannot be separated from each other. As Randall wrote in 1932,[97] salaries
were inadequate, but the librarian should not expect esteem
and rewards unless he met the standards of those with whom
he sought to identify. More bluntly, Vosper in 1957 stated
that many librarians want something for nothing; if they
proved themselves through scholarly activity and participation
in academic activities, they could achieve whatever they
wanted. Downs wrote that those who cannot or will not meet
qualifications established for the faculty should be excluded
from consideration for faculty status. [98]

Downs found in 1957 that library directors felt they
should establish high standards while at the same time striving to obtain faculty benefits for the professional staff. The
library administrators agreed on three points:

1. The maintenance of high standards for professional
staff appointments, in order to place the preparation of
librarians as nearly as possible on a par with their
colleagues in classrooms, and to insure top-notch library service to faculty and students.

2. Through academic status, equivalent rank, or special professional classification, to entitle librarians to

all appropriate rights, privileges, and perquisites received by the teaching faculty.

3. To obtain general acceptance and recognition of the
essential value of the librarians' contribution to the educational and research programs of the universities of
the country. [99]

Writing in 1955, Carlson thought some chief librarians unfortunately and complacently accepted conditions which relegated the professional staff to semi-clerical status. [100] Downs
looked with displeasure on those who ignored the plight of
their subordinates while demanding full faculty status for
themselves. [101] Judging from apparent lack of concern for
the staff welfare, Forgotson in 1961 intimated that some library administrators reveled in the superiority which an academic title gave them over their staff. [102]

Not until recent years have the benefits of faculty status become major issues and objectives for their own sake.
One successful effort by a staff association to gain full faculty status occurred in 1965, although the groundwork was
accomplished earlier. According to Harold Jones, success
in selling the concept requires a strong association, carefully formulated objectives supported by a substantial majority
of the membership, effective leadership, an emphasis on potential benefits to the institution, endorsement by faculty
groups, backing of chief librarians, and extensive efforts by
librarians. When success is achieved, faculty status must
be written into the by-laws or statutes governing the institution or system. [103]

On the national level, the Association of College and
Research Libraries (ACRL) recently formulated a proposal
which included censure and sanctions against institutions which
treated librarians unfairly. [104] Based on the "Status of Academic Librarians in California, " which in addition specified
that academic rank should not be directly related to administrative responsibility, [105] the ACRL resolution incorporates
demands both for the benefits of faculty status and for participation in academic government.

The emphasis on higher salaries and other benefits reflects a desire for personal gain on the part of practitioners,
but a concern about adequate compensation may also indicate
an attentiveness to the future of the profession. Branscomb
in 1940 thought that few faculty members would be willing to

forego their privileges and remuneration in order to accept a position as a librarian. To attract qualified people, he felt salaries and benefits for librarians had to be improved. [106] Wilson and Tauber believed in 1956 that some individuals would be drawn to librarianship because they were interested in the possibilities it offered. Nevertheless, most young people would compare its financial rewards with other professions and make a choice on the basis of potential rewards. [107] In 1961 Lyle saw efforts to improve salaries mainly as a means of attracting outstanding people. [108]

Cost can, of course, be a factor, as McAnally found in 1957. [109] More recently, the report on the status of the state college librarians in California, published in 1970, indicated that it may be some time before all the principles of the ACRL resolution are widely adopted. A special committee under the chairmanship of Robert Downs, appointed by William Dix, President of the American Library Association, recommended that librarians remain on 12-month contracts and raised questions about the research abilities and interests of librarians. It also questioned the concept of assigning rank without consideration for administrative duties. In substance the committee supported the principles of the ACRL resolution such as faculty rank, equal salary, tenure, voting rights, sabbatical leaves, and access to research grants; but it did not recommend immediate implementation because of the amount of money involved. [110]

Notes

1. Jane Forgotson, "A Staff Librarian Views the Problem of Status, " College and Research Libraries, 22 (July, 1961), 275. Henceforth, College and Research Libraries will be cited as CRL.

2. Bernard Barber, Social Stratification: A Comparative Analysis of Structure and Process (New York: Harcourt, Brace and World, Inc. , 1957), p. 41.

3. W. J. Reader, Professional Men: The Rise of the Professional Classes in Nineteenth-Century England (New York: Basic Books, Inc. , 1966), pp. 15-16.

4. Barber, Social Stratification, p. 41.

5. Ibid. , p. 25.

6. Ibid., pp. 24-27.

7. Joseph Ben-David, "The Growth of the Professions and
    the Class System," in Class, Status, and Power, ed.
    by Reinhard Bendix and Seymour Lipset (2nd ed.;
    New York: Free Press, 1966), p. 459.

8. Carl Hintz, "Criteria for Appointment to and Promotion
    in Academic Rank," CRL, 29 (September, 1968), 341.

9. George A. Works, College and University Library Prob-
    lems (Chicago: American Library Association, 1927),
    p. 81.

10. William M. Randall and Francis L. Goodrich, Principles
    of College Library Administration (2nd ed.; Chicago:
    American Library Association, 1941), pp. 30-33.

11. "Status of College Librarians in Texas," Library Journal,
    76 (March 15, 1951), 500-501. Henceforth Library
    Journal will be referred to as LJ.

12. Arthur M. McAnally, "The Dynamics of Securing Aca-
    demic Status," in The Status of American College and
    University Librarians, ed. by Robert B. Downs,
    ACRL Monograph, No. 22 (Chicago: American Library
    Association, 1958), p. 29.

13. Robert B. Downs, "The Current Status of University Li-
    brary Staffs," in The Status of American College and
    University Librarians, pp. 13-14.

14. Louis R. Wilson and Maurice F. Tauber, The Univer-
    sity Library (2nd ed.; New York: Columbia University
    Press, 1956), p. 322.

15. "Status of College and University Librarians," CRL, 20
    (September, 1959), 400.

16. Raj Madan, Eliese Hetler, and Marilyn Strong, "The
    Status of Librarians in Four-Year State Colleges and
    Universities," CRL, 29 (September, 1968), 382.

17. "Atlantic City Conference: A Great Show in Two Parts
    and a Cast of Thousands," ALA Bulletin, 63 (July-
    August, 1969), 952-53. The resolution is quoted
    above on pages 1 and 2.

18. Rice Estes, "Faculty Status in the City College Librar-
    ies, " CRL, 3 (December, 1941), 43.

19. Louis R. Wilson and Maurice F. Tauber, The University
    Library (2nd ed. ; New York: Columbia University
    Press, 1956), pp. 298, 322.

20. Guy R. Lyle, The Administration of the College Library
    (3rd ed. ; New York: H. W. Wilson Company, 1961),
    pp. 193-94.

21. "Status of College and University Librarians, " CRL, 20
    (September, 1959), 399.

22. Robert B. Downs, "Status of University Librarians--
    1964, " CRL, 25 (July, 1964), 253.

23. Madan, Hetler, and Strong, "The Status of Librarians in
    Four-Year State Colleges and Universities, " pp. 381-
    86.

24. W. E. Henry, "The Academic Standing of College Li-
    brary Assistants and Their Relation to the Carnegie
    Foundation, " Bulletin of the American Library Associ-
    ation, 5 (July, 1911), 261-62.

25. Works, College and University Library Problems, pp.
    81-83.

26. U. S. Office of Education, Survey of Land-Grant Colleges
    and Universities, directed by Arthur J. Klein, Bulle-
    tin, 1930, No. 9 (Washington, D. C. : Government
    Printing Office, 1930), 1, p. 689.

27. Miriam C. Maloy, "Faculty Status of College Librar-
    ians, " ALA Bulletin, 33 (April, 1939), 232.

28. Ibid. , pp. 233, 302.

29. Ibid. , pp. 232-33, 302.

30. James A. McMillen, "Academic Status of Library Staff
    Members of Large Universities, " CRL, 1 (March,
    1940), 138-39.

31. Morris A. Gelfand, "The College Librarian in the Aca-
    demic Community, " in The Status of American College

and University Librarians, pp. 151-52.

32. Frances L. Spain, "Faculty Status of Librarians in Col-
     leges and Universities of the South," in Southeastern
     Library Association, Papers and Proceedings, 13th
     Biennial Conference, Louisville, Ky., October 20-23,
     1948, pp. 45-53.

33. Lewis F. Stieg, "Retirement Plans for College and Uni-
     versity Librarians," CRL, 11 (January, 1950), 12.

34. Frank L. Schick, "Meet the College Librarian," LJ, 75
     (June 15, 1950), 1017-19.

35. Frank A. Lundy, "Faculty Rank for Professional Librar-
     ians," in The Status of American College and Univer-
     sity Librarians, pp. 144-45.

36. Robert H. Muller, "Faculty Rank for Library Staff Mem-
     bers in Medium-Sized Universities and Colleges," in
     The Status of American College and University Li-
     brarians, pp. 86-87.

37. Arthur M. McAnally, "The Dynamics of Securing Aca-
     demic Status," in The Status of American College and
     University Librarians, pp. 28-29.

38. Robert B. Downs, "The Current Status of University Li-
     brary Staffs," in The Status of American College and
     University Librarians, pp. 14-15.

39. Robert B. Downs, "Status of University Librarians--
     1964," CRL, 25 (July, 1964), 253-58.

40. Carl Hintz, "Criteria for Appointment to and Promotion
     in Academic Rank," CRL, 29 (September, 1968), 341-
     46.

41. Madan, Hetler, and Strong, "The Status of Librarians in
     Four-Year State Colleges and Universities," pp. 381-86.

42. Mary B. Cassata, "Teach-in: The Academic Librarian's
     Key to Status?" CRL, 31 (January, 1970), 22-27.

43. Gelfand, "The College Librarian in the Academic Com-
     munity," pp. 148-49.

44. Downs, "The Current Status of University Library
    Staffs," pp. 26-27.

45. McAnally, "The Dynamics of Securing Academic Status,"
    p. 37.

46. U. S. Office of Education, Survey of Land-Grant Colleges
    and Universities, directed by Arthur J. Klein, Bulle-
    tin, 1930, No. 9 (Washington, D. C.: Government
    Printing Office, 1930), 1, p. 690.

47. Downs, "The Current Status of University Library
    Staffs," pp. 19-25.

48. Anita R. Schiller, Characteristics of Professional Per-
    sonnel in College and University Libraries, Research
    Series No. 16 (Springfield: Illinois State Library,
    1969), pp. 68-69.

49. Donald P. Meyer, "An Investigation of Perceptions Re-
    garding the Instructional Function of the Library
    among Faculty Members and Librarians at Public
    Community Colleges in Michigan" (unpublished Ed. D.
    dissertation, Michigan State University, 1968), pp. 69-
    70.

50. Kaspar D. Naegele and Elaine C. Stolar, "The Librar-
    ian of the Northwest," in Libraries and Librarians of
    the Pacific Northwest, ed. by Morton Kroll, 4
    Seattle: University of Washington Press, 1960), pp. 64-
    66, 102-103.

51. Robert T. Blackburn, "College Libraries--Indicted
    Failures: Some Reasons--and a Possible Remedy,"
    CRL, 29 (May, 1968), 173.

52. Guy R. Lyle, The President, the Professor, and the
    College Library (New York: H. W. Wilson Company,
    1963), p. 31.

53. Kaspar D. Naegele and Elaine C. Stolar, "Income and
    Prestige," LJ, 85 (September 1, 1960), 2890.

54. Robert W. McEwen, "The Status of College Librarians,"
    in The Status of American College and University Li-
    brarians, pp. 171-75.

55. Harvie Branscomb, Teaching with Books (Chicago:
     American Library Association, 1940), p. 99.

56. Jane Forgotson, "A Staff Librarian Views the Problem
     of Status," CRL, 22 (July, 1961), 275-76.

57. Kevin Guinagh, "The Academic Image of the Librarian,"
     in The President, the Professor, and the College
     Library, pp. 11-13.

58. Peggy Heim and Donald F. Cameron, The Economics of
     Librarianship in College and University Libraries,
     1969-70: A Sample Survey of Compensations (Wash-
     ington, D. C.: Council on Library Resources, Inc.,
     1970), p. 3.

59. William M. Randall, The College Library: A Descriptive
     Study of the Libraries in Four-Year Liberal Arts Col-
     leges in the United States (Chicago: American Library
     Association, 1932), p. 51.

60. Robert Downs, "The Place of Librarians in Colleges and
     Universities," North Carolina Libraries, 18 (Winter,
     1960), 37-38. He expressed the same view in his
     "Are College and University Librarians Academic?"
     in The Status of American College and University Li-
     brarians, p. 78.

61. Patricia B. Knapp. "The College Librarian: Sociology
     of a Professional Specialization," in The Status of
     American College and University Librarians, pp. 58-
     59.

62. Delbert R. Farley, "The Image of the College Professor
     as Disclosed in General Magazines, 1938-1963" (un-
     published Ph. D. dissertation, Florida State University,
     1964); Eugene E. Hakanson, "The College Professor,
     1946-1965, As Revealed by an Analysis of Selected
     Magazine Articles" (unpublished Ed. D. dissertation,
     Indiana University, 1967); Frank W. Schufletowski,
     "The Development of the College Professor's Image in
     the United States from 1946-1964" (unpublished Ph. D.
     dissertation, Washington State University, 1966).

63. Tony B. Byles, "A Status Study of Teachers in Selected
     Colleges of Education in Louisiana" (unpublished Ed. D.
     dissertation, University of Southern Mississippi, 1963).

64. Harold F. Mackey, "A Study of the Prestige Associated
     with Selected Expectations Held for Members of the
     Resident Instructional Staff in a Land-Grant University"
     (unpublished Ph. D. dissertation, Washington State
     University, 1965).

65. Robert W. Hodge, Paul M. Siegel, and Peter H. Rossi,
     "Occupational Prestige in the United States, 1925-
     1963," in Class, Status, and Power, ed. by Reinhard
     Bendix and Seymour M. Lipset (2nd ed.; New York:
     Free Press, 1966) pp. 324-25.

66. Mary L. Bundy and Paul Wasserman, "Professionalism
     Reconsidered," CRL, 29 (January, 1968), 8.

67. Justin Winsor, "The College Library," in College Li-
     braries as Aids to Instruction, U. S. Bureau of Edu-
     cation, Circulars of Information, 1880, No. 1 (Wash-
     ington, D. C.: Government Printing Office, 1880),
     pp. 7-9.

68. Melvil Dewey, "The Profession," American Library
     Journal, 1 (September, 1876), 6.   This is volume 1
     of what later became Library Journal.

69. J. Periam Danton, "The Faculty, the Librarian and Book
     Selection," LJ, 61 (October 1, 1936), 715-17.

70. Robert P. Haro, "Book Selection in Academic Libraries,"
     CRL, 28 (March, 1967), 106.

71. Wilson and Tauber, The University Library, p. 425.

72. Ibid., pp. 425-48.

73. Lyle, The Administration of the College Library, pp.
     145-64.

74. McAnally, "The Dynamics of Securing Academic Status,"
     pp. 35-36.

75. Ibid., p. 36.

76. Maurice P. Marchant, "Faculty-Librarian Conflict,"
     LJ, 94 (September 1, 1969), 2886-89.

77. Blackburn, "College Libraries--Indicted Failures: Some Reasons--and a Possible Remedy," pp. 173-75.

78. Henry H. Scherer, "Faculty-Librarian Relationships in Selected Liberal Arts Colleges" (unpublished Ed. D. dissertation, University of Southern California, 1960), pp. 119-34.

79. McAnally, "The Dynamics of Securing Academic Status," p. 34.

80. Patricia B. Knapp, The Monteith College Library Experiment, (New York: Scarecrow Press, Inc., 1966), pp. 14, 130-43.

81. Guinagh, "The Academic Image of the Librarian," p. 17.

82. Felix Reichmann, "Hercules and Antaeus," in The Status of American College and University Librarians, p. 98.

83. McAnally, "The Dynamics of Securing Academic Status," p. 32.

84. William H. Carlson, "The Trend toward Academic Recognition of College Librarians," in The Status of American College and University Librarians, p. 67.

85. Frank A. Lundy, "Faculty Rank for Professional Librarians," in The Status of American College and University Librarians, pp. 112-13.

86. David C. Weber, "'Tenure' for Librarians in Academic Institutions," CRL, 27 (March, 1966), 99.

87. Marchant, "Faculty-Librarian Conflict," pp. 2888-89.

88. Branscomb, Teaching with Books, pp. 96-97.

89. Ibid., p. 197.

90. Humphrey G. Bousfield, "College Libraries with Dual Roles," CRL, 9 (January, 1948), 30.

91. D. L. Smith and E. G. Baxter, College Library Administration in Colleges of Technology, Art, Commerce, and Further Education (New York: Oxford University Press, 1965), p. 15.

92. Gelfand, "The College Librarian in the Academic Com-
    munity," pp. 146-47.

93. Ibid., p. 149.

94. Sidney H. Ditzion, "College Librarians and the Higher
    Learning," in The Status of American College and
    University Librarians, p. 157.

95. Works, College and University Library Problems, p. 81.

96. Muller, "Faculty Rank for Library Staff Members in
    Medium-Sized Universities and Colleges," pp. 88-89.

97. Randall, The College Library, pp. 59-60.

98. Downs, "The Current Status of University Library
    Staffs," pp. 22-23, 27. Vosper is quoted by Downs.

99. Ibid., pp. 25-26.

100. Carlson, "The Trend Toward Academic Recognition of
     College Librarians," p. 76.

101. Robert B. Downs, "Are College and University Librar-
     ians Academic?" in The Status of American College
     and University Librarians, pp. 81-82.

102. Forgotson, "A Staff Librarian Views the Problem of
     Status," pp. 278-79.

103. Harold D. Jones, "LACUNY: A Library Association in
     Action," California Librarian, 29 (July, 1968), 204-
     209.

104. "Atlantic City Conference: A Great Show in Two Parts
     and a Cast of Thousands," ALA Bulletin, 63 (July-
     August, 1969), 952-53.

105. "Status of Academic Librarians in California," Cali-
     fornia Librarian, 29 (January, 1968), 37-38.

106. Branscomb, Teaching with Books, p. 95.

107. Wilson and Tauber, The University Library, p. 297.

108. Lyle, The Administration of the College Library, p. 194.

109. McAnally, "The Dynamics of Securing Academic Status,"
     p. 32.

110. "Status of California State College Librarians,"
     American Libraries, 1 (January, 1970), 57-59.

Chapter 3

Problems and Responsibilities of Faculty Status

Many of the articles on faculty status for librarians
exhibit little acquaintance with the literature of other disciplines. If librarians want to enhance their position, it seems
imperative that they familiarize themselves with "the system" they are eager to join. A thorough comparison of criteria for appointments, promotion, and tenure of librarians
and faculty members could be of immense value to the profession. For present purposes, only a small portion of a vast
body of literature will be cited.

If librarians want faculty status, they must assume the
concomitant responsibilities. Among these education, research, and publication are primary considerations. In addition some writers attribute certain problems of attaining
faculty status to the fact that librarianship has been a feminine profession. At least to some extent, limited participation by librarians in faculty government may be related to
factors such as educational background, scholarly activity,
and sex; for all of these may to a degree determine acceptance by the academic community.

The Education of Academic Librarians

Probably the most significant considerations with regard to the education of librarians are: (1) the educational
standards of a profession are closely related to its status in
American society; (2) colleges and universities place considerable emphasis on degrees, especially the doctorate; and
(3) as various studies have shown, those librarians who have
the doctorate are virtually assured of high academic rank and
salary. For those who are seeking personal advancement or
an improved status for the entire profession, the education of
academic librarians should, then, be one of the central con-
cerns in the discussion of academic status.

Sociologists have found that educational requirements

are significantly and consistently related to the status which
a profession has achieved in American society. [1] The academic community, itself, values the doctorate.   According to
Wilson, the master's degree is no longer a badge of scholarship.   The person with the doctorate is expected to possess
a broad acquaintance with the field, a mastery of a special
topic, and research ability.   At major universities where the
doctorate may be expected, even at the instructor's level, the
title of professor carries more prestige, but in colleges and
lesser universities the title "doctor" may.   Furthermore,
where the doctorate may be expected at the instructor's level,
it is not a basis for promotion, whereas in many other institutions the degree itself may be a factor in determining rank.[2]
Discussing the education of university librarians in 1939,
Kerner, a professor of history, said that the doctorate is of
worth because it gives the individual "an intimate acquaintance
with the problems which scholars and competent students
meet in pursuing their work, " It develops an understanding
of the use of sources and their relationship.   With the doctorate the librarian would cease to be "merely a 'clerk'" or
"'an obstacle to scholars and scholarship.' "[3]   The respondents in Phoenix's 1965 dissertation on library administrators
indicated a "marked increase in respect" from the faculty,
students, and staff after they completed the doctorate. [4]

Speaking at a conference of the Midwest Academic Librarians, Russell Seibert, Vice-President for Academic Affairs at Western Michigan University, questioned whether librarians had met the educational and scholarly standards set
for the faculty and whether librarians should seek faculty
status without meeting those criteria. [5]

From the beginning of the twentieth century to the present time some librarians have stressed the need to raise the
educational level of the profession, but few precise guidelines
have been formulated.   Writing in 1911, Henry stated that librarians, if they wanted academic recognition, had to emulate
the faculty in scholarship and education, [6] and Williamson
emphasized the need for additional education for librarians, [7]
as did Klein in his 1930 report on land-grant colleges. [8]   Rec-
ognizing the value of subject knowledge in providing service,
the "Standards for College Libraries" in 1959 urged the desirability of a second or third master's degree. [9]   The Association of College and Research Libraries (ACRL) in 1959
recommended the master's as the first professional degree,
and implied that the criteria for librarians are the same as
those for faculty members. [10]   Kellam and Barker's 1968

statement, a preliminary draft for ACRL, was based on a
survey of members of the Association of Research Libraries
and other state university libraries. On the basis of the results the writers concluded that most faculty members have
or are working toward the doctorate, but most librarians do
not have that degree, nor do they need it. [11]

In summarizing the attitudes of faculty members
toward the education of librarians, Florence Holbrook said librarians are usually considered agreeable persons interested
in rendering good service; but what the faculty may want most
of all is intellectual capacity, creativity, and an understanding
of scholarship. She questioned whether pleasantness and co-
operativeness are adequate professional goals. [12] To Sidney
Ditzion the question of faculty status for librarians was an
issue because the professor deemed the librarian to be intel-
lectually inferior, [13] and Robert Downs, who has written more
extensively on the matter than anyone else, said in 1957 that
librarians must present equivalent qualifications if they want
recognition in the college or university as peers of teachers.[14]

In the future, college and university librarians will undoubtedly be called upon to have academic preparation as
thorough and as advanced as their colleagues in other
fields. [15]

More recently he asserted that librarians do not want to
cheapen the high standards for faculty appointments by insisting upon equal rank for unqualified candidates. [16] Madan,
Hetler, and Strong, in their study published in 1968, reit-
erated the admonition that librarians must willingly accept (as
opposed to having it forced upon them) the demand for equal
education and scholarly activity. [17] Thus practitioners themselves have placed great emphasis on this matter. At the
same time, however, McAnally writing in 1957 asserted that
minimal educational requirements were not always established
when seeking faculty status and that this might be a deterrent
to success. [18]

In what may be called the first full-length study of college and university library problems, Works was not sur-
prised to find that librarians were classified on the clerical
level in most colleges in view of the meager academic preparation of the professional staff in the institution he investigated. [19] Randall and Goodrich in 1941 wrote that no college
faculty should be expected to accept librarians as equals if
they were inferior in education or scholarship. They recom-

mended a minimum of a bachelor's degree plus an additional
year of study in library science and predicted that the time
was coming when the librarian would need the doctorate in
order to take his proper place on the campus.   Without the
appropriate credentials it would be difficult for the librarian
to earn recognition and respect and, therefore, cooperation.[20]
Talking about universities, Wilson and Tauber emphasized the
need for librarians with strong subject backgrounds and stated
that the doctorate was being demanded in more and more instances. [21] Although his study is more recent than those of
Works, Randall and Goodrich, or Wilson and Tauber, Lyle is
less decisive.   He simply reported existing practice, saying
that the usual requirement is a subject bachelor's and a
master's degree in library science.   However, he also was
willing to accept education and experience rated as equivalent
qualifications. [22]   This latter view has been espoused by other
writers, and the American Library Association itself put its
stamp of approval on the concept of "equivalent experience" in
its Classification and Pay Plans for college and university libraries.   Published in 1947, this document is presumably
now outdated, but it did represent an important, official statement of the Association.   Even for the highest positions in
college or university libraries the "minimum qualifications, "
to summarize briefly, in addition to experience, were a bachelor's plus three years of professional education including the
doctorate, or a bachelor's plus one year of study in a library
school and the doctorate in a subject other than library science, or a bachelor's plus two years of library science, or
a year of professional study beyond the bachelor's plus a
master's in another subject area, or one year of study in library science in addition to the possession of the bachelor's
degree, or equivalent experience. [23]

    A faculty member looking at this might conclude that
only the experience counts, not the education; and he might
speculate further that library science is after all a rather
simple subject which requires little if any formal, systematic
study.   But Wilson believed in 1947 that advanced study and
research in library science is more likely to insure competence and does this more systematically and quickly than pro-
longed experience. [24]

    Educational requirements are also, of course, related
to the specific tasks performed by the librarian.   Lyle would
have his cataloger engage in such activities as typing and
filing cards, handling processing details, and keeping statistics. [25]   And his librarian in charge of circulation "must spend

a great deal of his time" in such matters as charging and
discharging books, keeping records, and handling inter-library
loans. [26] Lyle did not suggest that the catalog or circulation
librarian has the responsibility to make sure that these tasks
are done well; the professional librarian himself engaged in
these routines. Wilson and Tauber recognized routine duties
as demanding much less background than is required for professional tasks; according to them, such duties as bibliographic searching, preliminary cataloging, and filing are all
clerical tasks in the cataloging department. [27]

As Downs has said a number of times, if librarians
want status, they also have certain responsibilities. One of
their first duties is to separate the clerical from professional
tasks. Obviously, he says, a master's degree is not required for checking in current periodicals, stamping date due
slips, shelving books, and many similar details. The ratio
of professional to clerical staff should be, according to the
suggestion of various writers, from one-third to one-half
professional, based on a careful analysis of positions. [28] To
place emphasis mainly or only on the technical aspects of librarianship, at the expense or virtual exclusion of the professional aspects related to the broad educational responsibilities of the librarian, is to relegate librarianship itself to
essentially a clerical level. Possibly it is this level of performance which writers like Parker had in mind when they
said that the librarian must be a scholar first, for it is
easier to teach technical knowledge to a scholar than it is to
make a scholar out of a technician. [29]

Librarianship has been criticized for its lack of a
"specialized body of knowledge" and because it does not require "long and intensive preparation. " Typical of the articles which propound this point of view is the editorial "Is
Librarianship a Profession?" which appeared in the California Librarian in July, 1964. [30] However, Hall's recent
doctoral dissertation should counter the arguments that the
profession lacks either the body of knowledge or the need
for long and intensive preparation.

Hall identified 83 areas of knowledge with which public
service librarians should be acquainted. Among these, six
were outside of the province of library school education:
knowledge of (1) a variety of subjects; (2) relationships between subject fields; (3) one subject area in some depth; (4)
general terminology in many fields; (5) foreign languages;
and (6) graphic information and language symbols. Thirteen

more, such as a knowledge of the community, of organizational structure of the library in which employed, and of
methods of operation peculiar to that institution, were related to the characteristics of a particular library. This left
64 which are of specific concern to library schools. She
singled out 20 of these for extensive examination. While it
is not necessary to examine or even list these in detail at
this point, it may be worth mentioning some of them. The
public service librarian needs to know literature in the broad
sense of that term, his clientele, institutions, principles of
planning and management, the technique of research, the ap-
plications and implications of automation, methods for effective communication, the tools of bibliographic searching, how
to find information, the principles of cataloging and classification, problems of selection, effective public relations procedures, and the purposes and functions of his type of library. [31] Such broad and extensive educational objectives as
those cited by Hall would seem to be enough, not just for the
doctorate but for lifelong study.

        If college and university librarians are inferior to the
faculty in academic preparation and scholarly achievement,
steps must be taken to remedy the situation, and ACRL
places much of the burden on the director. The head librarian has an obligation to adhere to high standards in appointment and promotion, and he must encourage continuing education. [32] In her 1957 dissertation on the professional development of reference librarians, Knox cited no examples of
effective programs for in-service education in college and
university libraries and found that little systematic attention
was being paid to this important area. [33] In a 1968 survey
of existing conditions of 64 members of the Association of
Research Libraries and 22 selected liberal arts colleges,
Jesse and Mitchell concluded that the directors were "receptive" to requests for time for formal study and worthwhile
research projects, but the "administrators contend, quite
rightly, that the individual librarian must take the initia-
tive. "[34] Hintz, in another survey in 1968, asserted that libraries had failed to establish standards of performance in
this area. [35] At the same time, it seems clear that some
emphasis on opportunities for further study is coming from
the rank and file. The librarians at the University of California at Berkeley, for example, have insisted upon time to
attend classes, access to research funds, sabbaticals, travel
funds, and fellowships;[36] and the Librarians Concerned about
Academic Status, a grass roots group, submitted a resolution
including some of these same principles at the American

Library Association Convention in Atlantic City in June, 1969. [37]

Previous Surveys on the Education of Academic Librarians

The Association of College and Research Libraries seems to imply that the educational level of librarians is already equal to that of the faculty, [38] and Downs also maintains that more and more librarians are earning doctorates.[39] Madan, Hetler, and Strong contend that the education of librarians has improved and that they have increasingly prepared themselves for full participation in the academic community, but that the increased qualifications have not resulted in greater recognition and reward. [40]

That the educational qualifications of librarians have definitely improved during the past 40 or 50 years can be shown by summarizing a selected number of studies on this question.   Table 2 details the degrees held by librarians as reported in various surveys from 1911 to the present.

TABLE 2

Highest Degrees of Academic Librarians
As Shown in Selected Previous Studies

Identification (date, author, inclusion)	No Degree	Bachelor's	Master's	Doc-torate
1911. Henry. 16 institutions	57%			
1927. Works. Department heads in 8 institutions	10. 3%	22. 6% professional; 48. 7% academic; 20. 5% both	12. 8%	
1930. Klein. Land-grant colleges and universities Head Librarians	22. 5%			

TABLE 2 Continued

Identification (date, author, inclusion)	No Degree	Bachelor's	Master's	Doctorate
1950. Kraus. Head librarians in 31 members of Assoc. of Amer. Univ. Head Librarians in 1933		17. 2%		20. 7%
Head librarians in 1948		96. 8% at least 1 yr. beyond B.A.		48. 4%
1953. Muller. 369 librarians in 49 medium-sized colleges and universities				5. 1%
1958. Morrison. 231 major executives earning more than $6,000 in 1958 and 476 minor and non-executives	1%	7% 21% BS in LS	7% 59% study beyond 1st professional degree	12%
1962. Caldwell. 471 directors of libraries with more than 50,000 volumes		2. 8% 42. 4% BS in LS	26. 9% 26. 3% 2 master's	18. 7%
1964. Pollard. 56 black chief librarians in the South		20% BS in LS	80% 14. 3% also advanced sub. degrees	3. 6%
1969. Schiller, 2265 U. S. librarians	1. 3%	9. 5% 12. 3% BS in LS	73. 3% 11. 6% had second master's	3. 6%

Note: In some instances the writer did not report statistics for certain degrees.

Realizing that faculty members attain rank partly as a result of their academic preparation, Henry in 1911 insisted that librarians should have equal qualifications because of the scholarly activities in which they are engaged. In order to gather information on the background of staff members, Henry surveyed 16 private and public universities in various parts of the country and found that only 43% of the librarians in those institutions had even a bachelor's degree. In one institution all librarians were considered faculty, but less than half of them had a degree. 41

Of greater value because he compared the academic preparation and salaries of department heads in libraries and assistant professors in eight institutions, Works' report in 1927 found that 54. 3% of the assistant professors had the doctorate, 3. 3% had a M. D., and 15. 7% had a master's degree. Among the librarians the highest degree was a master's, which was held by 12. 8% of the department heads. Nearly 49% had an academic degree, 20. 5% had both a professional degree and a degree in another subject area, and 10. 3% had no degree. Since Works thought that department heads should be equated with assistant professors for purposes of rank and salaries, these comparisons of the education of librarians and faculty members were critical. 42 Because of what he found, he concluded that the "heads of library departments could hardly be expected to be on the same salary basis, for equal periods of service, as assistant professors." Before this became feasible, the standards of preparation for department heads "would need to be set considerably higher than those represented by the institutions reporting. "43

In his 1930 Survey of Land-Grant Colleges and Universities, Klein was disturbed to discover that 22. 5% of the chief librarians did not have a bachelor's degree and that some 40% had no background in library science. He also believed strongly that librarians should be encouraged to continue their study after the bachelor's and first professional degree.

Why should librarians be the only members of a university faculty who almost universally discontinue their formal professional study after a year or two at a professional or graduate school?

He went on to say that librarians, like instructors, should

have "opportunities for graduate study without deduction from their salaries. "[44]

Klein was emphatic about the unfortunate consequences of placing low priorities on building a quality staff. In appointing anyone who could be hired for a minimal salary, the college or university administrator was directly inhibiting the effective development and utilization of the library. If the librarian was poorly qualified, Klein felt the rest of the staff would almost inevitably have even lower qualifications; for if the salary offered the chief librarian was so low as to permit the hiring only of someone with less than the bachelor's degree, the salaries and talent of those hired for subordinate positions would be even lower. [45]

The remaining surveys which will be summarized here can conveniently be divided into two groups: (1) a number of brief reports from the periodical literature, and (2) studies of the education of librarians which appear in various longer works, mainly master's theses and doctoral dissertations.

Kraus, in an article published in 1950, compared 31 head librarians of universities which were members of the Association of American Universities in 1948 with 29 holding the same position in 1933 and found considerable gains in educational background. In 1948, 15 or nearly half of the 31 had a doctorate, whereas in 1933, six of 29 held that degree. Likewise in 1948, 15 had a master's in a subject field compared with 12 in 1933, and 11 had a sixth-year library degree in 1948 compared with four in 1933. In 1948, 21 had at least a year of study in library science and five had no professional education, whereas in 1933, 12 had attended library school and 17 had no background in library science. Finally, in 1933, five had the bachelor's as the highest degree and one more was privately educated; in 1948 all but one had at least a year of study beyond the bachelor's. [46]

Muller's survey of 49 medium-sized colleges and universities in 1953 showed that of 369 staff members with rank and title, 167 were assistant professor or higher, and 70 were associate professor or higher, yet only 19 had a doctorate. He concluded, therefore, that factors other than education were taken into consideration in determining rank. While the doctorate was not essential for promotion to professor, it did seem to insure high rank. None of those who had that degree held rank of less than associate professor and 16 of the 19 were professors. [47]

Caldwell examined the biographies of 471 chief administrators of academic libraries with holdings of more than
50,000 volumes. He found that 13 held the bachelor's as the
only degree, 88 had a doctorate including 31 in library science, 211 had a master's degree in a subject, 200 had a
bachelor's in library science as the only library degree, 124
had both a subject master's and a degree in library science,
and 127 had only a master's in library science. [48] In her
study of 90 white and 56 black chief librarians in colleges in
the South, Pollard in 1964 reported that 80% of the black respondents held the master's degree and 20% held the bachelor's in library science. Thus all had earned at least one
professional degree. In addition to library science, slightly
more than 14% of the black respondents also held advanced
degrees in other subject areas; one of these had earned the
Ph. D. and another the Ed. D. Without citing figures Pollard
says that white chief librarians placed more emphasis on advanced degrees in academic disciplines, but blacks had more
professional preparation. [49]

Two important recent surveys contain sections on the
education of librarians. In Schiller's study of 2,265 academic
librarians, 13.5% had no library degree and another 2.9% had
only an undergraduate degree in library science. Thus, about
one-sixth lacked the basic professional degree, the master's
degree in library science. However, these figures are in-
fluenced by the fact that both in private institutions and junior
colleges librarians tended to possess a lower level of education; thus the percentages for public four-year institutions
would be somewhat improved. About 25% of Schiller's respondents held advanced degrees in subjects other than library
science. A total of 73.3% of 2,265 respondents had at least
a master's degree, and another 3.6% had a doctorate. As
Schiller pointed out, the number with the doctor's degree is
small when compared with the teaching faculty, but she adds
that the combination of the professional degree with other
graduate degrees is considered most desirable. About 11.6%
held such combinations. Another 12.5% were working toward
advanced degrees; of these, 36.1% of the men and 12% of the
women were working toward the doctorate. [50]

In 1958 Morrison studied 231 major library executives
earning $6,000 or more and a control group of 232 minor li-
brary executives and 224 other librarians without extensive
supervisory responsibilities. Because his was a select group
from the larger college and university libraries, one might
assume that his study would reflect the most highly educated

group in academic librarianship in the United States.

Of his major executives 81% had degrees beyond the basic professional degree, whereas less than 50% of the control group had that much education. Having the doctorate in librarianship was virtual assurance of major executive status and a subject doctorate was nearly so. Of the major executives 24%, of the minor executives 4%, and of the non-supervisory personnel 7% had a doctorate. Although it conferred a salary advantage, a subject master's alone had little influence in determining the selection of major executives. [51]

Examination of theses and dissertations on the education of librarians will be limited to two examples. Works such as Davidson's thesis on head librarians in liberal arts colleges in the South[52] or Parrott's on librarians in Who's Who in American Women, [53] which included academic librarians as well as those working in other types of libraries, or Goodrich's, which deals only with academic librarians in one state, [54] are excluded from present consideration.

Among the theses and dissertations in library science the first extensive study of the academic and professional preparation of college and university librarians was done by Zimmerman for his master's degree at the University of Illinois in 1932 (see Table 3). Of 260 head librarians in various type of institutions he found that 41 had no academic degree, 128 had a bachelor's, 65 had a master's, and 26 had a doctorate; 137 had no professional education, 69 had a year or less, and 54 had from one to two years. Thus just under 16% of the total had no degree. When the institutions were divided into three groups by size of from one to 599, 600 to 1,999, and over 2,000, he found that the librarians in the largest institutions had the highest degrees both in professional and academic areas, that librarians in the publicly supported institutions had a slightly higher level of education in both areas, and that there was a marked relationship between librarians with the doctorate and the large universities which usually had extensive graduate programs and professional schools. [55]

Bradley's master's thesis, completed in 1968, compared the qualifications of 50 directors of large academic and public libraries with their predecessors'. Of the predecessors in academic libraries, one had no degree, eight had the bachelor's, 18 had the master's, and 23 had the doctorate as the highest degree. Of the incumbents all had at least a

TABLE 3

Highest Degrees of Librarians Reported
in Theses and Dissertations

Identification (date, author, inclusion)	No Degree	Bachelor's	Master's	Doctorate
1932. Zimmerman. 260 head librarians	15. 7%	49. 2%	25%	10%
1969. Bradley. 50 predecessors and incumbent director of large academic libraries				
Predecessors	2%	16%	36%	46%
Incumbents	0	6%	40%	54%

baccalaureate, three had only the bachelor's, 20 had a master's, and 27 had the doctorate. Thus there is a definite increase in the level of education. In the incumbents' group only three rather than nine had the bachelor's or less, 20 rather than 18 had at least the master's, and 27 as compared with 23 in the earlier group had a doctorate. [56]

Both among the published works and in theses the differences between the educational level of librarians from the earlier period to more recent times is significant. In 1911 Henry's survey showed that 57% of the librarians had no degree whereas Schiller's 1969 report indicated that only 1. 3% of the professional librarians in all types of colleges and universities throughout the United States had no degree. At no time has a large percentage of all academic librarians held the doctorate. Because it included all professional librarians in all types of institutions, Schiller's study is the most useful in this regard, and she found that only 3. 6% held that degree.

Schiller states that academic librarians "have a high level of educational attainment. "[57] According to Morrison, the most conspicuous correlate of success as far as position and salary are concerned is the amount of education, and he showed that the education of academic librarians is considerably higher than that of business leaders, certified public accountants in California, and public librarians. [58] However, a "high level of educational attainment" is relative, and comparisons must be made with other groups to demonstrate comparative level. For academic librarians comparisons should be made with those with whom the librarians are seeking to identify, the faculty.

Unfortunately, none of these studies except Works' draws explicit comparisons between librarians and faculty members at the same institutions. However, statistics for the degrees of faculty members are available and may serve as some general basis for showing similarities or differences.

Tables 4 and 5 show the number of faculty members with the doctorate as reported in a number of different studies. In Berelson's most prestigious institutions 92% of the graduate faculty had the doctorate, which indicates that the degree alone is not essential to appointment even in the best institutions, and that other achievements such as publishing, research, and creative accomplishment may serve as acceptable substitutes for the degree. Nevertheless, his "best institutions" had the highest percentage of faculty members with the doctorate. Nearly all of the college presidents in his survey thought the research experience and writing of the dissertation were necessary or desirable for college teachers. [59]

Thus among the faculty the question of how many teachers have the doctorate is usually of considerable concern. One of the best summaries of the situation in recent times is that by Allan Cartter. During the period from 1953-54 to 1962-63 the percentage of those with the doctorate rose from 40.5% to 50.6% and Cartter believes this trend will continue. [60]

Consistently, then, more faculty members than librarians have had the doctorate. Only at the top administrative level in the large institutions, as shown in Bradley's study, has the percentage of librarians with the doctorate compared favorably with that for the faculty, although as Cartter's analysis showed, the percentage of doctorates among the faculty at different types of institutions also varies.

Incentives

Jordan, if he could create his ideal library-college,

TABLE 4

Percentage of Faculty Members with the Doctorate
as Shown in Selected Previous Studies

Identification (date, author, inclusion)	% with Ph. D.
1927. Works. Assistant professors in 8 institutions	54. 3
1960. Berelson. Graduate faculty in 12 best American universities	92
1965. Cartter. Full-time teachers in American colleges and universities	
1953-54	40. 5
1962-63	50. 6

TABLE 5

Percentage of Full-Time Faculty Members with the
Doctorate by Type of Institution in 1953-54
and in 1962-63

Type of Institution	1953-54	1962-63
Public universities	44. 0	58. 4
Private universities	51. 9	59. 6
Public colleges	30. 7	42. 6
Private colleges	35. 2	42. 7
All institutions	40. 5	50. 6

would eliminate all incentives and would abolish departments
and rank as these exist in American higher education today.
Except for a dependency allowance he would pay all his li-
brarian-teachers and teacher-librarians exactly the same
amount. [61]

Would such a system work? Three extensive recent
studies discuss means of encouraging continuing education.
According to Wallin, incentives have a significant impact on
the activities of faculty members, and a college or university
can to a marked degree influence what the faculty will or will
not do. For his study he selected two junior colleges which
were similar as far as the external environment was concerned but different in internal administrative factors. One
which he called Merit College used the traditional system of
faculty rank and salaries which were contingent upon education, professional activities, service to the institution, special activities such as counseling and serving as advisor to
student groups, and general contribution to the community.
The other institution labeled Non-Merit College had no academic rank nor career ladder and gave automatic salary increases without regard to the quality of performance.

The differences between the two institutions were evident both in staff morale and in contributions. Because
salary increments came automatically in Non-Merit College
without regard to performance, faculty members exhibited
less interest in professional development, they felt no one
cared about what they did, and they sometimes expressed
hostility toward the students who became a bother if they
needed or sought additional help. In Non-Merit College 37%
of the faculty members read professional journals regularly,
54% had attended conferences and seminars during the previous two years, and 54% participated in community activities. Even more important, none of the faculty members had
regular office hours although 10% said they did some counseling every week.

In Merit College faculty members had formal posted
schedules and spent an average of 5.5 hours each week in
counseling, 56% read professional journals, 82% had taken
advanced work in the previous two years, 74% had attended
conferences and seminars in the previous two years, and
67% participated in community activities. Furthermore,
teachers at Merit College thought the administration was interested in them as individuals, they knew what was expected
of them, and they devoted greater energies to participation in

such matters as counseling, study, and professional activities, all of which were valued and rewarded. Since the differences were marked in attitudes, morale, and time devoted
both to service to the students and to self-development, Wallin concluded that incentives are a critical factor in staff development. [62]

Knox's sample consisted of librarians in a university
in which they could remain at the instructor's level indefi-
nitely but without tenure. In addition to satisfactory job performance, publication, and professional activity, promotion
to assistant professor and eligibility for tenure required the
possession of either the doctorate or two master's degrees.
The desire for promotion in rank provided the major motivation for working toward advanced degrees. Other inducements were higher salary, an interest in personal improvement, and a desire to teach.

During the period from 1951-52 through 1955-56, 18
of the 22 librarians in Knox's sample took formal course
work toward advanced degrees. Three earned master's degrees, one earned a doctorate, and five took leaves of absence to work toward advanced degrees. The library itself
encouraged such activity by allowing three hours per week
for class attendance, and the librarian paid no fees. Leaves
of absence were granted freely, and the librarian could forego vacations for two years and then take the third summer
off at full pay. [63]

The recent work by Stone added a new dimension to
the question of the continuing education for librarians. The
assumption underlying her study is that librarians need additional education. It would then seem imperative that they establish standards and devise means to achieve the desired objectives, but standards alone are not the answer.

Possibly a large proportion of the librarians terminate
their education with the master's degree, according to Stone,
for they do not have the opportunity to work at a fully professional level. If the librarian is denied the chance to use
his ingenuity and accept responsibility, the consequence may
be frustration and apathy. Librarians felt substantial opposition from management regarding continuing education, and
many librarians thought they were capable of contributing far
more than their assignments permitted them to do.

As sources of encouragement for participation in pro-

fessional improvement activities she found that the most important factors were the quality of the activity itself, the
chance to learn new and creative ideas, and the opportunity
to use acquired knowledge on the job.   Those factors most
detrimental to participation were inferior quality of the activity, difficulties related to reaching the location of the activity, and lack of time or inflexible schedules.   As to formal
courses, motivation depended mainly upon the opportunity to
use the new knowledge on the job, high quality content, and
exposure to new and creative ideas. [64]

Publication and Research

Paul Woodring stated that about one percent of the
faculty will make distinguished contributions, another 10% will
publish regularly, 20% will publish occasionally, and 70% will
never publish after earning the doctorate. [65]   According to
Danton, librarians devote much time to helping research
workers in other fields, but they have not applied research
methods to librarianship. [66]

The question of how much time the teacher should devote to working with students and how much of his energy
should be devoted to the advancement of scholarship has received much attention.   Writers argue both for more and for
less research.

John Fischer, for example, decries what he calls the
wholesale desertion of the classroom by faculty members who
are hired as teachers but who gain recognition and prestige
as a result of publications, grants, prizes, or consultant-
ships.   Thus, he argues, the present system penalizes those
who conscientiously devote their energies to teaching and
working with students.   Because of the competition for those
who have reputations, the professor can establish his conditions of employment; but Fischer would have students, alumni,
foundations, and the government demand that institutions of
higher learning place restrictions on the faculty member's
activities.   The professor would have to devote his time and
energy to teaching rather than to research and consulting on
local, national, and international levels. [67]

According to Allen, scholarly activity itself is an important factor in determining prestige both within the department and within the profession.   The senior professor may
win the esteem of his colleagues and students, not because of

his academic rank and title, but as a result of contributions to his field. [68] Further, the requirements for success within a profession demand contributions which are visible to the audience beyond the confines of a particular institution. The good teacher is rarely known beyond the gates of his own college or university, but the writer may gain international acclaim. [69] Through publication the professor submits his ideas to the scrutiny of other specialists in the field who are often the only ones competent to judge the merits of his contribution. [70]

To some extent the emphasis on research is based on the premise that quality teaching is associated with research and publication. Donald Orlich, for example, maintained on the basis of observation and personal experience that

> those who do not write and those who are not actively engaged in some research at some plane are, more often than not, those professors who, as teachers, have the least to offer. This does not mean that all research men are great teachers, but that the odds are in their favor. [71]

Others argue that there is no relationship between the quality of teaching and publication when sufficient time has been allotted for teachers to engage in both. [72] Nevertheless, Roy Francis affirms that the professor who publishes is not only teaching in the classroom but also provides the means for other teachers to keep up with the field. Thus the writer is performing an especially vital function. He dares to presume that he can teach the teachers, and this task, according to Francis, may be the most significant form of teaching. [73] Since a good teacher must inspire curiosity, Hans Schmitt questions whether the professor who lacks the necessary curiosity to engage in continuing investigation can generate adequate motivation and interest in his students. Also, the teacher needs respite after covering essentially the same material year after year and listening to the same response from students. Without a change afforded by research, he argues, the teacher will stagnate. [74]

According to Woodburne, the importance of research has seldom been rightly understood by the American public.

> It is in no sense a luxury that can be done away with in times of stress. For research and scholarly work are the very substance of progress in ideas, in science, in

human affairs.   As a dean of a law school remarked,
'scholarship provides the material for the textbooks of
the next decade. ' In this sense the results of scholarly
study are essential for inspired teaching. [75]

If the professor could refashion the world to his own
liking, he would place instruction first, then would come
scholarly activities and publication, next he would choose research sponsored by outside sources.   He would drastically
curtail his administrative and other university duties, and
put least emphasis on professional activities and services
outside of the university. [76]

Few articles discuss the importance and need for research by librarians in a vein similar to the discussions of
the academicians cited above.   Tyler says the question of
whether graduate professional education should develop
scholars or better practitioners has been a concern of most
professions. [77] Kellam and Barker suggest that most librarians do not have an interest in research and writing, nor
should they be expected to engage in it as extensively as
does the faculty.

It is true that most librarians are required to follow a
relatively inflexible schedule which cannot be relaxed to
any great extent without causing service to suffer. . . .
Probably librarians as a group should not be expected
to engage in most of these activities--for example, research and consultation--to the same extent as the faculty....   Many librarians have neither the interest to do
extended research nor should it be expected of them because of the nature of their work....   The library must
accept as its main function responsibility for providing
the materials of scholarship and research to students,
faculty, and scholars. [78]

Much of the low prestige librarians enjoy in the academic community may result from attitudes such as those
expressed above.   Are the excuses of lack of time and the
assertion that librarians should be content with serving the
scholarly needs of others convenient, conscience-salving excuses for those who lack the imagination to devise alterna-
tives?   Dare librarians expect scholars from other disciplines to undertake the necessary research into the pressing
problems of libraries?   Shera is one of those who believes
that librarians must place much more emphasis on research.
They have not even made a substantial beginning toward

finding answers to the critical questions of how and why
people use books and what influence books exert on the
reader. [79]   According to Daniel Bergen, academic librarians,
unlike teachers, tend to have a strong institutional orientation, and unless they engage in scholarly activity their recognition will come almost exclusively from the institutional,
administrative status system. [80]

   A number of studies have shown that publication increases the librarian's opportunities.   Morrison found that
93% of his male and 71% of his female major executives had
published as compared with 68% of the men and 54% of the
women in his control group.   Although this was more pronounced among men than among women, he also reported a
strong relationship between the number of publications and
the level of position and salary. [81]   It seems apparent that
those who publish become known in the profession through
writing and are therefore more likely to be considered and
selected for major executive posts. [82]   As far as evaluation
and promotion within the same library is concerned, Madan,
Hetler, and Strong found that work performance, advanced
degrees, and seniority were all considered more important
than research and publication. [83]   Similarly Hintz implied
that scholarly activity should not be a major criterion for
promotion because only a small percentage of librarians
meet faculty standards in this regard.   He added that more
librarians would probably engage in such activities if it were
clearly understood that it was expected of them.   Furthermore, on the basis of results in his survey, he suggested
that librarians who have faculty status are more likely to
meet faculty standards than those who are in some ill-de-
fined position. [84]

Participation in Academic Government

   Writing on the administration of institutions of higher
learning, Williams in 1965 said that faculty committees are
of value mainly because they constitute channels of communication.   From the point of view of the central administration, faculty committees can provide a means of generating
understanding and support, and for the faculty they can insure avenues for discussion of faculty needs and interests. [85]
In spite of their importance, Woodburne in 1958 considered
committee and administrative work "a minor, but relevant"
factor in judging a faculty member's contribution. [86]

Writing in 1957, Robert Downs thought eligibility for
service on academic committees was not of major significance, [87] but other librarians tend to hold a different view.
Membership on academic and other college or university
committees, Moriarty maintained in 1970, is a measure of
acceptance by the faculty and the administration.   It is an
important concomitant of faculty status because the librarian
must know his community if he is to be able to render
effective service, and committee work provides one means
of keeping in touch.   He believes that librarians are often
regrettably and deliberately ignored when appointments are
decided for important committees. [88]   Lyle held in 1945 that
the librarian needed a greater degree of intellectual attainment and more personality than did a faculty member to
gain membership on important educational and policy making
committees. [89]

Partly because of their service orientation, librarians,
according to Holbrook, are eager to serve on academic committees, and this also gives them an overt sense of identification with the faculty. [90]   But this desire for greater in-
volvement might strike faculty members as foolhardy.   Theophilus found that many teachers would like to drastically
curtail their administrative and committee responsibilities. [91]

While a number of studies have discussed the librarians' participation in committee work, two may be cited as
indicative of the trend in acceptance of librarians as members of the faculty.   Reporting on the results of his study
of 50 liberal arts colleges, teachers colleges, and small
universities in the East in 1948, Gelfand wrote that few
members of the library staff served on academic committees; and one respondent explained this on the basis of sex,
the faculty being mainly male and the library staff mainly
female.   Also, because some of the librarians did not have
faculty status, one would not expect them to be on any academic committees.   Surprisingly, only 30% of the head librarians served on library building committees in those institutions which had such a body, and only 52% thought it
was important for the librarian to be a member of that committee.   While 90% served on the library committee, 80%
thought it was of major consequence to be a member.   Even
among the head librarians Gelfand found negligible representation in such areas as the curriculum, publications, graduate, research, personnel, and budget committees. [92]

Gelfand's respondents in 1948, then, seemed to exhibit comparatively little interest in committee work. By way of contrast Kellam and Barker's study showed that progress had been made by 1968; 98% or nearly all of the 72 directors of the Association of Research Libraries and state universities reported that staff members served on academic committees ranging from the housekeeping level, such as parking, to more critical ones such as those on media, computer centers, publications, and area studies programs. The writers did not state what proportion of the staff served on committees, but they did "give the impression that the number varies considerably" at different institutions. Nevertheless, they implied that participation by librarians on academic committees is substantial. [93] In any case, participation in committee work seems to have changed considerably between Gelfand's 1948 report and that of Kellam and Barker in 1968, and Moriarty is more insistent about the librarian's voice in academic government than were the respondents in Gelfand's survey. That librarians want to participate in academic government is also borne out by the 1969 resolution of the Association of College and Research Libraries which calls for a direct voice by librarians in the college or university's decision making processes. [94]

Professional Activity

        The reason for encouraging participation in professional activities, as Harrington and Lyle state, is that this has a direct effect on the individual's ability to render effective service. [95] Such involvement provides a means of keeping abreast of developments in the field through exchanging views with other librarians, seeing new equipment and books, and attending meetings and hearing papers read. [96] As the Educational Policies Commission pointed out, Americans have become joiners. They have formed all types of groups from recreational and social to religious, labor, professional, and managerial associations. Belonging to professional associations should be of value because the association supports high standards of service, seeks to improve the qualifications of its members through continuing education, and is dedicated to advancing knowledge. The association performs services which the individual cannot accomplish on his own. Participation is one way of demonstrating professionalism by showing dedication to the principles for which the organization stands. The association itself has a responsibility to encourage research and disseminate information through publication and sponsorship of activities such as conferences and workshops. [97]

Librarians in Morrison's sample, with an average of 5. 3 memberships, belonged to more scholarly and professional associations than did public librarians or college graduates in general. Furthermore, active participation in these associations was directly related to salary and position. Only 3% reported no membership in associations. [98]

As Morrison indicated, academic librarians appear to hold more memberships in professional organizations than most other librarians. Blayton's 1960 study of 1, 146 catalogers in the 1955 edition of Who's Who in Library Service found that 25. 6% of the men and 16. 1% of the women did not belong to any associations. [99] In his study of 50 directors of large academic libraries, Bradley found that only 8% did not belong to national library associations, [100] which may support Morrison's finding that head librarians tend to belong to more professional associations than do other staff members.

Possibly librarians place more emphasis on professional activities than do college and university administrators. Woodburne, for example, maintained that membership on regional or national committees and association memberships in general are not major indications of accomplishment and should not therefore be of much consequence in evaluating the individual for promotion. [101]

Sex

Librarianship in the United States in the twentieth century has typically been identified as a feminine profession, and some writers have attributed its major problems to that factor. It is probably unique among the professions in that it was once predominantly male, then was taken over almost entirely by female practitioners, and now is again attracting a larger number of men.

Table 6 shows the percentage of male and female librarians from 1870 to 1960 as reported in the U. S. census. In 1870 approximately one of every five librarians was a woman (20. 2%). [102] The percentage of women increased rapidly. By 1900 nearly three of every four (74. 5%), [103] and by 1930 well over nine of every ten were women (91. 4%). [104] By 1940 the percentage of men had increased

TABLE 6

U. S. Census Figures on Male and Female Librarians

Year	Men		Women	
	Number	Percent	Number	Percent
1960	12, 045	14. 3	71, 836	85. 7
1940	3, 801	10. 5	32, 546	89. 5
1930	2, 557	8. 6	27, 056	91. 4
1900	1, 059	25. 5	3, 125	74. 5
1870	170	79. 8	43	20. 2

so that men represented slightly more than one of every ten
(10. 5%), [105] and by 1960 approximately one of every seven
librarians was a man (14. 3%). [106]

According to Rider, only ten women were listed
among the 156 attendants at the first meeting of the American Library Association in 1876. Melvil Dewey had much
to do with bringing an increasing number of women into the
profession. Upon being appointed librarian at Columbia University, Dewey brought in six young women to work in the
library. His intransigence about admitting females to the
library school when it opened in 1887 caused his brush with
the trustees of Columbia University, who insisted that women
should not be admitted to what was then an all male institution. Consequently, when he moved to Albany in 1889, Dewey
took the library school with him. [107] According to Sable,
especially during the depression of the 1930's when salaries
of librarians were too low to support a family, women virtually took over the public library. However, since World
War II a larger number of men have been entering the profession, [108] a contention supported by Naegele and Stolar who
also maintain that men have a better chance of getting the
top administrative positions. [109]

In his book published in 1939, Munthe stated that the
feminization of any profession results in low salaries; and
he added that considering the preparation required, librarianship was one of the most inadequately paid of all occupations. He also saw in this the danger that the situation was
self-perpetuating. Salaries were too low to attract men and

salaries would not rise until more men came into the profession. [110]

Both Blackburn[111] and Marchant[112] have suggested
that some of the conflicts between faculty members and librarians may result from the fact that most faculty members are men whereas most librarians are women.   Marchant suggests that as more men enter the profession they
will exhibit greater aggressiveness regarding such matters
as faculty status and privileges.

A number of other studies support the assertions of
Blackburn and Marchant.   While a striking resemblance
seemed to exist between academic women and female librarians, Holbrook concluded that women in general tend to be
more intelligent but less self-asserting than men. [113]
Borchers, in a symposium on the education of women, stated
that women in college teaching appear to be unwilling to re-
sist discrimination in such matters as rank and salary. She
also maintained that women are more likely to be prejudiced
against female administrators than are men. [114]   Similarly,
Adair, in his study of 415 librarians and library science
students, found that the men in his sample tended to be
more individualistic and somewhat more rebellious than the
women.   In general the male librarians were similar to
business executives and male college students although the
librarians were inclined to be slightly more intellectual,
flexible, and feminine.   Of course, femininity in males may
be considered an undesirable trait by many in American
society, but it is generally found to a greater degree among
men in American intellectual life. [115]

Traditionally, women have received less pay for similar work and the gap appears to be increasing.   From 1957
to 1968 the average income of full-time male workers rose
from $4,713 to $7,800, an increase of 65%, whereas for
women it rose from $3,008 to $4,550, an increase of 51%.
Furthermore, the number of women in legislatures and congress declined substantially between 1960 and 1968.   Whether
the Women's Liberation Movement will influence women to
become more self-assertive remains to be seen.   The 1964
Civil Rights Act included a provision against discrimination
in employment on the basis of sex, and about 7,500 com-
plaints against unfair treatment to women have been brought
before the Equal Employment Opportunity Commission. [116]

As shown in Table 7, the percentage of male academic

TABLE 7

Percentage of Male and Female Librarians
in Selected Previous Studies

Identification (date, author, inclusion)	% Men	% Women
1932. Randall. Head librarians in 205 liberal arts colleges	25	75
1961. Seeliger. Librarians in Who's Who in America, 1956-57	74	26
1967. Blankenship. Colleges with enrollments of 5,000 or less	48.5	51.5
enrollments of 1,501-5,000		
public colleges	66.7	33.3
private colleges	58.7	41.3
private colleges enrollments under 500	36.1	63.9
1968. Bradley. 50 large academic libraries		
predecessors	92	8
incumbents	100	0
1968. Ingraham.		
University Library Directors	93	7
Public College Libraries	64	36
Private College Libraries	48	52

TABLE 8

Percentage of Male and Female Faculty Members in
American Colleges and Universities as Reported in 1961

Identification (date, author, inclusion)	% Men	% Women
1961, Pfnister. Faculties in 255 colleges and 29 universities		
Total Sample	74.1	25.9
Universities	88.2	11.8
Liberal arts colleges	68.2	31.8
Junior colleges	65.6	34.4
Teachers colleges	64.6	35.4

librarians has increased considerably from the 1930's to the
1960's.   In 1932 Randall found that even among head librarians, women outnumbered men by three to one in the 205
liberal arts colleges he studied.   However, men were more
likely to be heads of the larger libraries and in positions
which paid a higher salary. [117]

Davidson, in his 1936 study of liberal arts colleges
in the South, reported that more men than women head librarians had faculty status and that men held the positions
in the better colleges, but he explained the differences by
indicating that the advantage of the male resulted from more
education and from more publishing. [118]

In a recent study based on 414 responses from colleges with enrollments of fewer than 5,000 students, Blankenship found that 48.5% of the head librarians were men, but
again, men were more likely to hold the director positions
in the larger libraries.   When the institutions were grouped
by size, 66.7% of the directors were men in the larger
publicly supported colleges with enrollments of from 1,501 to
5,000 students, and 58.7% in the privately supported ones of
the same size.   In the private colleges with enrollments
under 500, 36.1% of the librarians were men. [119]   Blankenship's figures represent a considerable increase in the percentage of men in the total sample as compared with Randall's findings in 1932.

That men have consistently tended to hold more of the
administrative positions in the larger libraries is substanti-
ated by the studies cited above, but in the major university
libraries the dominance of men is even more marked.
Among 50 incumbents and predecessors who were directors
of large university libraries, Bradley found that four of the
predecessors and none of the incumbents were women. [120]
Since being listed in Who's Who in America is to some extent the result of the position held by the biographee, it is
not surprising that Seeliger found nearly three times as
many men (319) as women (112) librarians in the 1956-57
edition.   However, it is also worth noting that more than
ten times as many of the men (83) as compared with the
women (8) held a doctorate.

Indicative of the kind of librarian one might expect to
find in the "Who's Who" type of publication is the fact that
317 (73.5%) of the 431 librarians held administrative positions.   Of these 317, 239 (75.4%) were men.   Four times

as many men (172) as women (43) were associated with academic libraries or library schools. [121]

In his Mirror of Brass, published in 1968, Ingraham reported that 93% of the directors of university libraries were men.   Only in private colleges were men a minority with 48%. [122]

Among college and university teachers in the United States women have always been in the minority.   Pfnister in 1961 reported that 25.9% of the teaching faculty in his survey were women (see Table 8) but he found much variation by type of institution.   In universities 11.8% of the faculty members were women compared with 31.8% in liberal arts colleges, 34.4% in junior colleges, and 35.4% in teachers colleges. [123]   Thus, among faculty members as among librarians, men have an advantage as far as the more highly regarded positions are concerned.

As for possible discrimination, it must be pointed out that differences exist between men and women in education and publication as well as in rank and salary.   Pfnister's survey showed that 53.5% of the men had a doctorate as compared with 23.2% of the women faculty members. [124] According to David Brown, women tend to be lower in academic rank, have fewer degrees, earn less, and publish less than men.   However, he asserted that discrimination exists in spite of the achievement of the individual female.   Thus if she has the doctorate and has published extensively, a woman still has less chance of getting a position in a prestigious university, for example.   Also, it is worth noting that 41% of the faculty at the women's colleges were women; yet these institutions, according to Brown, discriminated against women teachers more than did the coeducational institutions.

But Brown also maintained that much of the apparent discrimination is self-imposed; that is, women prefer to accept positions at those institutions which place less emphasis on research in spite of the fact that this means both a heavier teaching load and lower salaries.   Furthermore, he reported a Pennsylvania State University study which found that female teachers are more effective with the low ability and average students but less successful with superior students.   He concluded that women tend to seek positions in institutions where they are likely to make the greatest contribution, and the present allocation of teaching abilities and resources may be the most desirable possible.

In summary, Brown stated that at least four arguments have been advanced to explain the differences in salary
and rank between men and women faculty members: (1)
Women publish less than do men;   (2) A smaller percentage
of the women faculty members have the doctorate;   (3)
Women choose to go to those institutions which place less
emphasis on research and publishing and conversely more
emphasis on teaching;   (4) Women tend to be concentrated in
the lower paying disciplines and in the lowest paying region,
the North Atlantic states. [125]

As far as salary and position are concerned another
important factor needs to be considered.   Schiller pointed
out that those women who are married are less mobile than
men and may accept whatever level of position and remuneration is offered.   The librarian who is willing to move is
likely to have both a better salary and higher position.   Thus
mobility itself contributes to the differences in salary and
rank between men and women. [126]

The opportunity to learn has considerable influence on
what people do learn in contrast to what they can learn, and
women, according to Carrington's study, have fewer opportunities to learn.   Encouragement is an important factor in
determining whether women will pursue graduate study, and
family responsibilities were the most frequently cited reason
for not doing so.

In her study of senior women in the Southeast, Carrington found that 35% of the seniors planned to enter graduate school, but only 12% enrolled in the following academic
year.   Among those who had planned to continue their education, marriage, cited by 24. 5% of the female respondents,
was the reason given most frequently for not enrolling.
Those who did go had above average grades but had also discussed plans more frequently with faculty members and had
been singled out by faculty members who had offered unso-
licited encouragement.

Of itself the monetary advantage of an advanced degree was not a strong motivating factor nor was family income a strong determinant.   To put it in positive terms,
women in Carrington's sample went to graduate school because of an interest in the subject and in the chosen profession. [127]   In a 1963 Wisconsin symposium on the education

of women, Borchers reported that women are less likely to get financial support from parents when a choice must be made between supporting a son or daughter in college; and women also receive fewer research grants, fellowships, scholarships, and assistantships. [128]

Although age might be treated separately, it is in general related to sex. Thus it would seem appropriate to discuss it in this connection. Because, even among women with the doctorate, one quarter leave the labor force, and because the homemaker role affects their professional commitment, Brown suggests that women are considered a greater gamble by many colleges and universities. [129] Since many of them drop out of the labor force while their children are young, women who work tend on the average to be older than men. Schiller's study, which serves as a good example, found that the largest percentages of men were in the 30 to 50 age span, but for the women the largest percentages were below 30 and above 45. According to Schiller this is consistent with conditions in other professions. [130]

In summary then, the literature indicates that the high proportion of women in the profession would seem to have serious implications for librarians: (1) Fewer women earn the doctorate; (2) they are less interested in research and publishing; (3) they are less self-assertive; (4) they are less concerned about status and salary; (5) they are less mobile than men which makes them less competitive for salaries and positions; and (6) they are to some extent victims of both unwarranted and self-imposed discrimination.

Notes

1. Bernard Barber, Social Stratification: A Comparative Analysis of Structure and Process (New York: Harcourt, Brace and World, Inc., 1957), pp. 40-41.

2. Logan Wilson, The Academic Man: A Study in the Sociology of a Profession (New York: Oxford University Press, 1942), pp. 38-42, 114.

3. Robert J. Kerner, "Essentials in the Training of University Librarians--IV," CRL, 1 (December, 1939), 33-34.

4. William D. Phoenix, "The Doctorate and the University

Library Administrator" (unpublished Ph. D. dissertation, University of Missouri at Kansas City, 1965),
p. 172.

5. Russell H. Seibert, "Status and Responsibilities of Academic Librarians, " CRL, 22 (July, 1961), 253.

6. W. E. Henry, "The Academic Standing of College Library Assistants and Their Relation to the Carnegie
Foundation, " Bulletin of the American Library Association, 5 (July, 1911), 259-61.

7. Charles C. Williamson, Training for Library Service:
A Report Prepared for the Carneigie Corporation of
New York (New York: 1923), pp. 123-24.

8. U. S. Office of Education, Survey of Land-Grant Colleges
and Universities, directed by Arthur J. Klein, Bulletin, 1930, No. 9 (Washington, D. C.: Government
Printing Office, 1930), 1, pp. 682-83.

9. "Standards for College Libraries, " CRL, 20 (July, 1959),
276.

10. "Status of College and University Librarians, " CRL, 20
(September, 1959), 400.

11. W. Porter Kellam and Dale L. Barker, "Activities and
Opportunities of University Librarians for Full Par-
ticipation in the Educational Enterprise, " CRL, 29
(May, 1968), 199.

12. Florence Holbrook, "The Faculty Image of the Academic
Librarian, " Southeastern Librarian, 18 (Fall, 1968),
177.

13. Sidney H. Ditzion, "College Librarians and the Higher
Learning, " in The Status of American College and
University Librarians, ed. by Robert B. Downs,
ACRL Monograph, No. 22 (Chicago: American Library
Association, 1958), p. 156.

14. Robert B. Downs, "The Current Status of University Library Staffs, " in The Status of American College and
University Librarians, p. 27.

15. Robert B. Downs, "Are College and University Librar-

ians Academic?" in The Status of American College and University Librarians, p. 84.

16. Robert B. Downs, "The Place of Librarians in Colleges and Universities," North Carolina Libraries, 18 (Winter, 1960), 41.

17. Raj Madan, Eliese Hetler, and Marilyn Strong, "The Status of Librarians in Four-Year State Colleges and Universities," CRL, 29 (September, 1968), 386.

18. Arthur M. McAnally, "The Dynamics of Securing Academic Status," in The Status of American College and University Librarians, pp. 36-37.

19. George A. Works, College and University Library Problems (Chicago: American Library Association, 1927), pp. 82-89.

20. William M. Randall and Francis L. Goodrich, Principles of College Library Administration (2nd ed.; Chicago: American Library Association, 1941), pp. 120-122.

21. Louis R. Wilson and Maurice F. Tauber, The University Library (2nd ed.; New York: Columbia University Press, 1956), pp. 261-78.

22. Guy R. Lyle, The Administration of the College Library (3rd ed.; New York: H. W. Wilson Company, 1961), pp. 188-92.

23. American Library Association, Board on Personnel Administration, Classification and Pay Plans for Libraries in Institutions of Higher Education: Vol. 3: Universities (Chicago: American Library Association, 1947), pp. 156-58.

24. Louis R. Wilson, "Historical Development of Education for Librarianship in the United States," in Education for Librarianship, ed. by Bernard Berelson (Chicago: American Library Association, 1949), pp. 54-55.

25. Guy R. Lyle, The Administration of the College Library (New York: H. W. Wilson Company, 1945), p. 95. The job description is similar in the 1961 edition except that the cataloger no longer typed cards. See

        pp. 69-70 of the 1961 edition.

26.   Lyle, The Administration of the College Library, 1961,
       p. 103.

27.   Wilson and Tauber, The University Library, p. 278.

28.   Downs, "Are College and University Librarians Aca-
       demic?" pp. 83-84.

29.   Wyman W. Parker, "College-Library Personnel," Li-
       brary Quarterly, 24 (October, 1954), 354-55.

30.   "Is Librarianship a Profession?" California Librarian,
       25 (July, 1964), 163-65.

31.   Anna C. Hall, Selected Educational Objectives for Pub-
       lic Service Librarians: A Taxonomic Approach (Uni-
       versity of Pittsburgh, 1968), pp. 29-98.

32.   "Status of College and University Librarians," CRL,
       20 (September, 1959), 400.

33.   Margaret E. Knox, "Professional Development of Re-
       ference Librarians in a University Library: A Case
       Study" (unpublished Ph. D. dissertation, University of
       Illinois, 1957), pp. 2-5.

34.   William H. Jesse and Ann E. Mitchell, "Professional
       Staff Opportunities for Study and Research," CRL, 29
       (March, 1968), 87-100.

35.   Carl Hintz, "Criteria for Appointment to and Promotion
       in Academic Rank," CRL, 29 (September, 1968), 345.

36.   "Berkeley Library Union States Bargaining Terms,"
       LJ, 93 (October 15, 1968), 3736.

37.   "Atlantic City Conference: A Great Show in Two Parts
       and a Cast of Thousands," ALA Bulletin, 63 (July-
       August, 1969), 925-26, 952-53.

38.   "Status of College and University Librarians," CRL,
       20 (September, 1959), 400.

39.   Downs, "Are College and University Librarians Aca-
       demic?" pp. 79-80.

40. Madan, Hetler, and Strong, "The Status of Librarians
     in Four-Year State Colleges and Universities, " p.381.

41. Henry, "The Academic Standing of College Library
     Assistants and Their Relation to the Carnegie Founda-
     tion, " pp. 258-63.

42. Works, College and University Library Problems, pp.
     88-90.

43. Ibid., p. 89.

44. U. S. Office of Education, Survey of Land-Grant Col-
     leges and Universities, p. 682.

45. Ibid., pp. 684-89.

46. Joe W. Kraus, "The Qualifications of University Li-
     brarians, 1948 and 1933, " CRL, 11 (January, 1950),
     17-21.

47. Robert H. Muller, "Faculty Rank for Library Staff
     Members in Medium-Sized Universities and Colleges,"
     in The Status of American College and University
     Librarians, p. 91.

48. John Caldwell, "Degrees Held by Head Librarians of
     Colleges and Universities, " CRL, 23 (May, 1962),
     227-28, 260.

49. Frances M. Pollard, "Characteristics of Negro College
     Chief Librarians, " CRL, 25 (July, 1964), 281-83.

50. Anita R. Schiller, Characteristics of Professional Per-
     sonnel in College and University Libraries, Research
     Series No. 16 (Springfield: Illinois State Library,
     1969), pp. 30-41.

51. Perry D. Morrison, The Career of the Academic Li-
     brarian, ACRL Monograph, No. 29 (Chicago: Ameri-
     can Library Association, 1969), pp. 23-24, 39.

52. Chalmers G. Davidson, "The Status of Librarians in
     Southern Liberal Arts Colleges" (unpublished Master's
     dissertation, University of Chicago, 1936).

53. Shirley Parrott, "An Analysis of the Biographies of

Librarians Listed in Who's Who of American Women,
1958-1959" (unpublished Master's thesis, Atlanta
University, 1962).

54. Charlotte G. Goodrich, "Faculty Status of Professional
     Library Personnel in Ohio Collegiate Institutions"
     (unpublished Master's thesis, Kent State University,
     1952).

55. Lee F. Zimmerman, "The Academic and Professional
     Education of College and University Librarians" (un-
     published Master's thesis, University of Illinois,
     1932), pp. 7-8, 88-91.

56. Ben W. Bradley, "A Study of the Characteristics,
     Qualifications, and Succession Patterns of Heads of
     Large United States Academic and Public Libraries"
     (unpublished Master's report, University of Texas,
     1968), pp. 75, 79, 82.

57. Schiller, Characteristics of Professional Personnel in
     College and University Libraries, p. 30.

58. Morrison, The Career of the Academic Librarian,
     pp. 15, 23.

59. Bernard Berelson, Graduate Education in the United
     States (New York: McGraw-Hill Book Company, Inc.,
     1960) pp. 52, 127-28.

60. Allan M. Cartter, "A New Look at the Supply of Col-
     lege Teachers," Educational Record, 46 (Summer,
     1965), 267-77.

61. Robert Jordan, "The Library-College—A Merging of
     Library and Classroom," in The Library College:
     Contributions for American Higher Education, ed. by
     Louis Shores, Robert Jordan, and John Harvey (n. p.:
     Drexel Press, 1966), p. 59.

62. Herman A. Wallin, Faculty Input: A Function of a Col-
     lege's Incentive System (Eugene, Oregon: University
     of Oregon, Center for the Advanced Study of Educa-
     tional, Administration, 1966), pp. 6-13.

63. Margaret E. Knox, "Professional Development of Re-
     ference Librarians in a University Library: A Case

Study" (unpublished Ph. D. thesis, University of
Illinois, 1957), pp. 118-19.

64. Elizabeth W. Stone, Factors Related to the Professional
     Development of Librarians (Metuchen, N. J. : Scare-
     crow Press, Inc. , 1969), pp. 201-213.

65. Paul Woodring, "The Profession of College Teaching, "
     Journal of Higher Education, 31 (May, 1960), 280-81.

66. J. Periam Danton, "Doctoral Study in Librarianship in
     the United States, " CRL, 20 (November, 1959), 440.

67. John Fischer, "Is There a Teacher on the Faculty?"
     Harper's Magazine, February, 1965, pp. 18-28.

68. Donald F. Allen, "Changes in the Role of the American
     University Professor" (unpublished Ph. D. dissertation,
     University of Texas, 1962), pp. 222-23.

69. Wallin, Faculty Input, p. 1.

70. David Riesman, "The Academic Career: Notes on Re-
     cruitment and Colleagueship, " Daedalus, 88 (Winter,
     1959), 160.

71. Donald C. Orlich, "Universities and the Generation of
     Knowledge, " Education, 88 (September-October, 1967),
     83.

72. Robert W. Beard, "On the Publish-or-Perish Policy, "
     Journal of Higher Education, 36 (November, 1965),
     456.

73. Roy G. Francis, "Publication and Academic Merit, "
     Modern Language Journal, 51 (November, 1967),
     391-94.

74. Hans A. Schmitt, "Teaching and Research: Companions
     or Adversaries, " Journal of Higher Education, 36
     (November, 1965), 419-27.

75. Lloyd S. Woodburne, Principles of College and Univer-
     sity Administration (Stanford, Calif. : Stanford Univer-
     sity Press, 1958), pp. 60-61.

76. Donald R. Theophilus, Jr. , "Professorial Attitudes

toward Their Work Environment at The University of
Michigan: A Study of Selected Incentives" (unpublished
Ph. D. dissertation, The University of Michigan, 1967),
pp. 127-29.

77. Ralph W. Tyler, "Educational Problems in Other Professions," in Education for Librarianship, ed. by
Bernard Berelson (Chicago: American Library Association, 1949), pp. 29-30.

78. W. Porter Kellam and Dale L. Barker, "Activities and
Opportunities of University Librarians for Full Parti-
cipation in the Educational Enterprise," CRL, 29
(May, 1968), 199.

79. Jesse H. Shera, "The Role of the College Librarian--
A Reappraisal," in Library-Instructional Integration
on the College Level, ACRL Monograph, No. 13
(Chicago: Association of College and Reference Libraries, 1955), p. 10.

80. Daniel P. Bergen, "Librarians and the Bipolarization
of the Academic Enterprise," CRL, 24 (November,
1963), 469.

81. Morrison, The Career of the Academic Librarian,
pp. 63-64.

82. John F. Harvey, "Advancement in the Library Profession," Wilson Library Bulletin, 36 (October, 1961),
146.

83. Madan, Hetler, and Strong, "The Status of Librarians
in Four-Year State Colleges and Universities,"
pp. 385-86.

84. Carl Hintz, "Criteria for Appointment to and Promotion
in Academic Rank," CRL, 29 (September, 1968),
344-45.

85. Robert L. Williams, The Administration of Academic
Affairs in Higher Education (Ann Arbor: The University of Michigan Press, 1965), pp. 4-6.

86. Woodburne, Principles of College and University Administration, p. 69.

87. Downs, "The Current Status of University Library
     Staffs, " p. 18.

88. John H. Moriarty, "Academic In Deed, " CRL, 31
     (January, 1970), 14-17.

89. Lyle, The Administration of the College Library, 1945,
     p. 263.

90. Holbrook, "The Faculty Image of the Academic Librar-
     ian, " p. 188.

91. Theophilus, "Professorial Attitudes toward Their Work
     Environment at The University of Michigan: A Study
     of Selected Incentives, " p. 129.

92. Morris A. Gelfand, "The College Librarian in the Aca-
     demic Community, " in The Status of American Col-
     lege and University Librarians, pp. 149-50.

93. Kellam and Barker, "Activities and Opportunities of
     University Librarians for Full Participation in the
     Educational Enterprise, " pp. 197-98.

94. "Atlantic City Conference: A Great Show in Two Parts
     and a Cast of Thousands, " ALA Bulletin, 63 (July-
     August, 1969), 925-26, 952-53.

95. Roseanne H. Harrington and Guy R. Lyle, "Recruiting
     and Developing a Library Staff, " CRL, 8 (October,
     1947), 435.

96. Wilson and Tauber, The University Library, pp. 311-12.

97. Educational Policies Commission, Professional Organi-
     zations in American Education (Washington, D. C.:
     Educational Policies Commission, National Education
     Association, 1957), pp. 4-35.

98. Morrison, The Career of the Academic Librarian,
     pp. 59-60.

99. Reida D. Blayton, "A Study of the Characteristics of
     Professional Catalogers as Indicated in Who's Who in
     Library Service, 1955" (unpublished Master's thesis,
     Atlanta University, 1960), p. 21.

100. Bradley, "A Study of the Characteristics, Qualifica-
     tions, and Succession Patterns of Heads of Large
     United States Academic and Public Libraries, " p. 98.

101. Woodburne, Principles of College and University Ad-
     ministration, p. 82.

102. U. S. Secretary of the Interior, Ninth Census of the
     United States, 1870: Population, 1, pp. 676, 686.

103. U. S. Department of the Interior, Census Office,
     Twelfth Census of the United States, 1900: Popula-
     tion, pt. 2, p. 505.

104. U. S. Department of Commerce, Bureau of the Census,
     Fifteenth Census of the United States, 1930: Popu-
     lation, 5, General Report on Occupations, p. 20.

105. U. S. Department of Commerce, Bureau of the Census,
     Sixteenth Census of the United States, 1940: Popu-
     lation, 3, The Labor Force, pt. 1, p. 75.

106. U. S. Department of Commerce, Bureau of the Census,
     Eighteenth Census of the United States, 1960, 1,
     Characteristics of the Population, pt. 1, p. 534.

107. Fremont Rider, Melvil Dewey (Chicago: American Li-
     brary Association, 1944), pp. 44-51, 78-82.

108. Arnold P. Sable, "The Sexuality of the Library Pro-
     fession: The Male and Female Librarian, " Wilson
     Library Bulletin, 43 (April, 1969), 748-49.

109. Kaspar D. Naegele and Elaine C. Stolar, "The Li-
     brarian of the Northwest, " in Libraries and Librar-
     ians of the Pacific Northwest, ed. by Morton Kroll,
     4 (Seattle: University of Washington Press, 1960),
     p. 128.

110. Wilhelm Munthe, American Librarianship from a
     European Angle: An Attempt at an Evaluation of
     Policies and Activities (Chicago: American Library
     Association, 1939), pp. 155-60.

111. Robert T. Blackburn, "College Libraries--Indicted
     Failures: Some Reasons--and a Possible Remedy, "
     CRL, 29 (May, 1968), 173.

112. Maurice P. Marchant, "Faculty-Librarian Conflict, "
      LJ, 94 (September 1, 1969), 2887.

113. Holbrook, "The Faculty Image of the Academic Li-
      brarian, " p. 182.

114. Gladys L. Borchers, "Some Investigations Concerning
      the Status of Faculty Women in American Colleges
      and Universities, " in Women in College and Univer-
      sity Teaching: A Symposium on Staff Needs and
      Opportunities in Higher Education, ed. by Joseph V.
      Totaro (Madison: University of Wisconsin, School of
      Education, 1963), p. 17.

115. Fred L. Adair, "The Development of a Scale to Mea-
      sure the Service Orientation of Librarians: Prelimi-
      nary Investigations" (unpublished Ph. D. dissertation,
      University of North Carolina, 1968), pp. 45-58.

116. "The New Feminists: Revolt Against 'Sexism, '" Time,
      November 21, 1969, pp. 53-56.

117. William M. Randall, The College Library: A Descrip-
      tive Study of the Libraries in Four-Year Liberal
      Arts Colleges in the United States (Chicago: Ameri-
      can Library Association, 1932), p. 63.

118. Davidson, "The Status of Librarians in Southern
      Liberal Arts Colleges, " p. 126.

119. W. C. Blankenship, "Head Librarians: How Many Men?
      How Many Women?" CRL, 28 (January, 1967),
      42-43.

120. Bradley, "A Study of the Characteristics, Qualifica-
      tions, and Succession Patterns of Heads of Large
      United States Academic and Public Libraries, " p. 18.

121. Ronald A. Seeliger, "Librarians in Who's Who in
      America, 1956-1957" (unpublished Master's thesis,
      University of Texas, 1961), pp. 23, 31, 119.

122. Mark H. Ingraham, The Mirror of Brass: The Com-
      pensation and Working Conditions of College and
      University Administrators (Madison: University of
      Wisconsin Press, 1968), p. 199.

123.   Allan O. Pfnister, A Report on the Baccalaureate
       Origins of College Faculties (Washington, D. C.:
       Association of American Colleges, 1961), pp. 41-42.

124.   Ibid., p. 43.

125.   David G. Brown, Academic Labor Markets (Chapel
       Hill, N. C.: n. p., 1965), pp. 164-69.

126.   Schiller, Characteristics of Professional Personnel in
       College and University Libraries, pp. 46-48.

127.   Dorothy H. Carrington, "An Analysis of Factors
       Affecting the Decision of College Women Seniors of
       the Southeast to Enter Graduate School" (unpublished
       Ed. D. dissertation, Florida State University, 1961),
       pp. 19, 35-42, 81-93.

128.   Borchers, "Some Investigations Concerning the Status
       of Faculty Women in American Colleges and Uni-
       versities, " p. 17.

129.   Brown, Academic Labor Markets, pp. 165-67.

130.   Schiller, Characteristics of Professional Personnel in
       College and University Libraries, pp. 21-22.

Chapter 4

Benefits of Faculty Status

This chapter reviews discussions of the major benefits of faculty status including: (1) faculty rank, (2) sabbaticals and other leaves, (3) commensurate salaries, (4) tenure,
(5) time and financial support for research and writing, and
(6) travel funds. Of these benefits faculty rank is a critical
concern, for it is a measure of identification with the teaching staff and raises questions about the qualifications for
academic rank. At the same time, commensurate salaries
are of considerable interest to librarians. Since arguments
regarding the librarian's eligibility for faculty status are
closely related to his background and contribution, much of
the material presented in the previous chapters is, of course,
also applicable to the issues examined here.

Academic Rank

The idea that the head librarian should have the rank
of professor, the associate librarian (an administrative position just below the director) that of associate professor, and
the other members of the staff that of instructor or assistant
professor depending on abilities, education, and position was
proposed at least as long ago as 1911. In making this recommendation Henry insisted that only those who are qualified
should be accorded faculty rank; those who did not meet
faculty standards should not be considered members of the
professional staff. [1] Works in 1927 drew comparisons between directors of large libraries and deans and between directors of smaller libraries and heads of academic departments. He felt that the associate librarians should be
equated with associate professors and department heads in
libraries with assistant professors. [2]

Although other writers have also discussed the question of the appropriate rank for librarians, no carefully
formulated policy has been developed as to how librarians
should be distributed among the various academic ranks. In

1940 McMillen deemed it inadvisable to appoint librarians
with the first professional degree at the rank of instructor
in those institutions which had higher requirements for faculty members at the lowest rank. [3]   Randall and Goodrich in
1941 recommended a professorial rank for the chief librarian, but only if he was qualified for that rank and salary by
virtue of his preparation and achievement. [4]   Similarly,
Moriarty in 1970 discussed the problems of rank, promotion,
and tenure which arise from the fact that most librarians
have only the master's degree. [5]

Of course, considerable differences in assigning rank
exist between the smaller colleges and universities and the
leading universities in the country.   In many smaller institutions the faculty member without the doctorate is appointed
as instructor, but those with the doctorate usually receive
the rank of assistant or associate professor. [6]   As has been
stated by writers such as Woodburne, teaching is usually the
primary consideration for promotion in the liberal arts college, but in a major university the situation is more complex.   There the faculty member is judged by his degrees
and his influence on students but also by his participation in
learned societies, his reputation among other scholars in the
field, and his publications.

Normally at the university, Woodburne continues, appointment to the rank of instructor requires the appropriate
professional preparation, and in many fields this is the doctorate plus a promise of competence in research and teaching.   Promotion requires evidence of progressive achievement, and the rank of professor should be reserved for those
"who, in the opinion of their colleagues, are outstanding,
mature scholars and who have earned national recognition."[7]
The identification of academic rank with the scholar-teacher
has led some writers, like Ingraham, to express concern
about the possible blurring of distinctions, and he would
rather abolish academic rank than destroy its meaning by
extending it to those who do not meet the requirements. [8]

Because of the standards for the appointment and promotion of faculty members and because of the traditional
meaning of academic rank as viewed by men such as Ingraham, faculty rank is one of the more complex and sensitive
issues which librarians encounter in seeking faculty status.
It often becomes a question of whether librarians have the
appropriate credentials.   Hintz, on the basis of 70 replies
from members of the Association of Research Libraries and

other institutions, mainly state universities, concluded that librarians can and do meet faculty criteria for appointment and promotion, and more would if position descriptions required them to do so. It is worthy of note, too, that he found definite indications that librarians were more likely to meet faculty standards in those institutions at which they had faculty status. Consequently, it appears that granting faculty status to librarians directly benefits the institution by encouraging librarians to pursue advanced study and research.[9] To cite a particular instance, Ralph Ellsworth, Director of Libraries at the University of Colorado, reported a marked increase in scholarly activities after the library staff received faculty titles. [10]

Although the evidence may not be conclusive, Hintz's and Ellsworth's statements indicate that librarians with faculty status are more likely to meet faculty standards than those who are in a separate classification.

Sabbaticals and Other Leaves

Sabbatical leaves as defined by Eells include four essential elements. Ordinarily, (1) the recipient must propose some self-improvement project, (2) he receives partial salary for a full year or full salary for half a year, (3) he must have served the institution for a stipulated number of years, and (4) he incurs an obligation to return for at least a year after the leave. Harvard University established the first such system in 1880. By 1900, nine additional institutions had such plans, and before 1920, 50 colleges and universities had them. [11] Currently the typical system allows full salary for half a year or half salary for a full year, but many variations exist. [12]

"An adequate program of leaves is considered among the most important benefits that an institution provides. "[13] Ingraham found that both teachers and administrators support this view. Effective plans contribute both to the recruitment and retention of faculty members, and he put leaves along with retirement policies and major medical insurance in the most valuable category of fringe benefits. In universities the chief use of leaves is for research and writing or for study to refurbish the scholar rather than for work toward a degree. In some of the smaller, less prestigious institutions the major purpose of sabbatical leaves is to support study toward advanced degrees.

The number of leaves granted each year may be
limited by lack of funds or by staffing requirements.   Although 80% of Ingraham's institutions reported that funds
were usually adequate, budgetary considerations were a determinant of how many individuals could get a leave at any
given time. [14] Of 22 institutions which reported actual ex-
penditures in 1956-57, sabbatical leaves cost an average of
$33, 603. [15]

A special committee of the American Association of
University Professors discussed the problem of cost.   Many
institutions have limited or no sabbatical leave programs because funds set aside for this purpose must necessarily
compete with budget requirements for salaries and other
fringe benefits such as retirement and insurance, and occasionally with buildings and campus beautification.   Nevertheless, because leaves are one of the best means of enhancing
a teacher's or scholar's effectiveness, the institution should
look upon sabbaticals as an investment in the individual, in
its own future, and in a larger sense as a contribution to
society.   Furthermore, the institution should "use its funds
to equalize the means of professional development among the
various fields and even within each field. "[16]

Because policies regarding leaves and the use of funds
differed and because definitions were not uniform, Ingraham
said that his findings had to be interpreted with some caution.   With these reservations in mind he reported that in
745 colleges and universities answering the question, 2. 1%
of the total faculty were on sabbaticals, 2% were on leaves
without pay, . 8% were on leaves other than sabbaticals but
supported by institutional funds, and . 5% were on leaves under
special grants.   Thus 5. 3% of the total faculty in 1962-63
were on leave.   Publicly supported colleges were below the
average with a total of 4. 1% on leave, and he explained this
partly on the assumption that these institutions had a high
percentage of faculty members who were comparatively new
members of the staff and were therefore not eligible for
leaves.

In all, 57% of the institutions reported sabbatical
leave plans.   In addition, 60% of the universities and somewhat under 40% of the colleges granted leaves other than
sabbaticals with pay.   Nearly all universities apparently
granted leaves when these were supported by special grants,
as did about 40% of the colleges.   About one-third of the
institutions granted leaves to instructors but about 15% ex-

cluded instructors and assistant professors.   In some institutions the applicant had to have tenure before he became
eligible. [17]   In 1962 Eells reported much diversity in practices at the 48 institutions which were among the first to
establish sabbatical leave plans.   In some, only professors
were eligible; in others, professors and associate professors,
all professorial ranks, all ranks, both the faculty and academic staff, or only those with the doctorate. [18]

      Table 9 gives statistics from a number of reports on
the eligibility of librarians for sabbatical leaves.   In his
Mirror of Brass, based on replies from 877 colleges and
universities throughout the United States, Ingraham reported

TABLE 9

Eligibility of Librarians for Sabbatical Leaves
in Selected Previous Studies

Identification (date, author, inclusion)	% of institutions with sabbatical leave plans	% of institutions in which librarians are eligible
1958. Boughter. 150 colleges in North Central Assoc.	56	47
1968. Ingraham. 877 colleges and universities	60	38
1968. Jesse and Mitchell. 52 universities	75	52
1968. Madan. 183 state colleges and universities	(no report)	79. 8
1970. Wright. 65 academic libraries	(no report)	54

that over 60% of the institutions had sabbatical leave plans
by 1966.   Librarians were eligible on the same basis as
faculty members in 38% but, with the exception of graduate

deans, other administrative officials received even less favorable treatment than librarians. With regard to leaves
without pay only a slightly higher 42% of the librarians were
eligible, yet they were again surpassed only by graduate
deans at 57%. Of those administrators who had been in
their positions for more than ten years, graduate deans
(44%) were highest in percentage of those who had taken
leaves and librarians were second (42%). Both groups were
above presidents, vice-presidents, liberal arts deans, business officers, deans of students, admissions officers, registrars, and development officers. The average faculty
member was likely to receive about twice as much leave
time as the average administrator. Four-fifths of the librarians and graduate deans were eligible for certain leaves
on the same basis as faculty members, and these groups
were again above any other administrative group. Among librarians, business officers, deans of students, registrars,
directors of development, and admission officers, the most
common reason for taking leaves was to pursue graduate
study, and this mainly because many of them did not have
the doctorate. [19] As an indication of the number of faculty
members on leave at a given time, a National Education Association report found that in 168 state colleges 421 faculty
members were on leave to pursue advanced study, and 297
were on leave for other reasons in 1960-61. This represented 3.9% of the entire faculty at these institutions. Others
no doubt worked toward advanced degrees during the summer. [20]

     In studies limited to librarians, Wright reported in
his 1970 survey of 65 academic libraries that 54% were eligible for sabbaticals on the same basis as faculty members,
but he added that librarians put more emphasis on vacations,
sick leave, faculty rank, and salaries than on sabbaticals. [21]

     Writing in 1958, on the basis of 150 replies from col-
leges with enrollments between 500 and 2,000 and accredited
by the North Central Association, Boughter found that 56% of
the institutions had sabbatical leave plans. Librarians were
included in 47%. Discrimination against librarians occurred
most often in private colleges. [22] In a 1968 article Madan,
Hetler, and Strong reported that librarians received unequal
treatment with regard to sabbaticals in 20.2% of the 183
state colleges and universities surveyed. [23] Jesse and
Mitchell found that 39 of the 52 universities in their sample
granted sabbaticals, but librarians were eligible in only 27.
In eight of these, all librarians were eligible; in 11, eligi-

bility was dependent upon the rank held by the individual;
and in most of the remaining eight, eligibility was determined on the basis of the position held. Although their questionnaire did not permit a detailed analysis of how extensively librarians took advantage of this privilege, and in spite
of the fact that the respondents did not always distinguish
between sabbaticals and other leaves, Jesse and Mitchell's
discussion would seem to indicate that the librarians took advantage of this opportunity where it was available. As might
be expected, however, leaves with pay were the more popular. [24]

With regard to leaves other than sabbaticals conditions are more favorable. Jesse and Mitchell in 1968 stated
that 80% of the university libraries in their sample granted
such leaves. [25] In the same year Kellam and Barker reported a slightly higher figure, with 82% of the university libraries granting leaves of absence on a basis similar to that
for the faculty. [26]

In assessing existing conditions with regard to sabbaticals and other leaves several points should be kept in
mind: (1) Many colleges and universities do not have a system of leaves with pay for any employees, and those institutions which have plans often have limited funds to support the
program. (2) Librarians are not always eligible on the same
basis as faculty members. (3) Although it may be more in
the nature of some slight solace without contributing to a
solution of the issue, librarians in general receive more favorable treatment in this regard than do presidents, academic deans, business managers, registrars, admission
officers, development officers, and deans of students. (4)
The previous studies show variation in the percentage of librarians eligible. In 1968 Ingraham, for example, reported
that 38% of the head librarians were eligible for sabbaticals
on the same basis as the faculty; and Madan, Hetler, and
Strong found that 79.8% of the librarians in state colleges
and universities were treated equally with faculty members.
Jesse and Mitchell found that only 52% of the librarians in
large universities were eligible. Some of the differences
reflect divergent practices in different types of institutions,
but discrepancies may also result to some extent from the
lack of accord on the definition of the various types of leaves.

Commensurate Salaries

Salaries have been a perennial concern. Ditzion
thought in 1947 that one of the primary motivations behind
the discussion of the status of librarians was to devise a
means of gaining equal salaries. [27]   Muller's 1953 questionnaire, covering 49 medium-sized colleges and universities,
showed that salaries for librarians without administrative
responsibilities were generally lower on a 12-month basis
than those for instructors on nine months. He thought this
might be related to the shortage of librarians. [28]   Similarly,
Lyle wrote in 1961 that salaries for librarians were lower
than for faculty members in private institutions with enrollments of more than 1,000. [29]

Historically it would seem that the only member of
the staff to receive reasonably adequate compensation has
been the chief librarian, for this view has been expressed
by a number of writers, among them Carlson in 1946[30] and
Wilson and Tauber in 1956. The latter placed great emphasis on salaries which were competitive with other occupations as a means of attracting qualified people into the
profession, for they considered personnel the "key to administration."[31]   By way of contrast, Lyle, writing in 1961,
felt that few librarians "enter--or should enter--the library
profession to make money; ideals for the most part must be
the determinant." Such ideals included an

> unshakeable belief in the importance of books, an am-
> bition to make books easily and conveniently available
> to readers, and a faith in the ability of librarians to
> share with others the task of bringing readers to books.[32]

At the same time he maintained that the level of remuneration of the library staff was a measure of the value the institution placed on the library. Like Wilson and Tauber, he
believed that salaries had to be improved to induce outstanding people to become librarians. [33]

Two sociologists, Naegele and Stolar, in their 1960
study of librarians in the Pacific Northwest, discovered some
discontent with salaries, but it tended "to be tame and gen-
teel." Furthermore, with librarians as with other salaried
professionals, concern with income

> is related to certain notions of self-respect (and the de-
> gree to which one believes that an institution's willing-

ness to pay is an indication of that institution's recognition of one's worth). [34]

In general the librarians seemed to be more concerned about being good librarians and about their personal betterment in salary and prestige than about launching a crusade to improve conditions for the entire profession. For those who were dissatisfied the usual admonition was to change positions "or keep quiet about it. "[35]

Because they have not made a concerted, unified drive for greater tangible rewards, librarians have been accused of being timid by many writers including Sellers[36] and Jones. The latter also showed that a carefully planned course of action supported by a substantial majority of the librarians in a public university system can result in substantial gains. In the City University of New York librarians won more than a 20% increase in salary and all faculty benefits as a result of aggressive, group action. [37]

Among faculty members salary ranges are usually quite broad to permit the rewarding of those with advanced degrees and special abilities. Ingraham stated that the scale from the lowliest full-time teacher to the most accomplished professor was often a multiple of four or five. [38] Williams in 1965 cited examples of both discrete and overlapping salary ranges. In those institutions which have discrete salary ranges the lowest salary for an assistant professor was more than the highest salary for the instructor, the lowest for an associate professor was above the highest for an assistant professor, etc. Other institutions have overlapping scales in which the salary for the highest paid instructors extends into the range for assistant professors, and the same holds for other ranks.

Remuneration for the highest paid professors, according to Williams, may be three to four times that of the beginning instructor. Within the rank of professor, the top salary may be twice or nearly twice that of the lowest salary for that rank. Naturally, great variations exist among institutions. Some colleges and universities hire faculty members without the doctorate, others normally expect that degree at the instructor's level in some disciplines. Consequently comparisons among institutions must be made with caution. [39]

Although published in 1927, Works' study is significant

because it is one of the few which made explicit comparisons between librarians and faculty members. He noted,
for example, that only two of 11 reporting institutions paid
department heads in libraries a salary which on the average
equalled or exceeded that of assistant professors. Considering the length of service per year increased the disparities, for most of the librarians worked 12 months while the
teaching faculty usually worked nine. [40] Because the education of the assistant professor was considerably higher than
it was for the department heads in the library, Works concluded:

> From the above statement of the situation, heads of li-
> brary departments could hardly be expected to be on the
> same salary basis, for equal periods of service, as
> assistant professors. The standard of preparation would
> need to be set considerably higher than those repre-
> sented by the institutions reporting. [41]

From 1910 to 1925 salaries for librarians rose more
dramatically than those for teachers (see Table 10). The
head librarians' salaries rose 207% while professors' rose
163. 6%. For the department heads in libraries, salaries
rose 202. 2% while assistant professors' rose 156. 8%. [42]

TABLE 10

Salaries of Librarians and Faculty Members: 1910 and 1925

Position	1910	1925	% Increase
Head Librarians	$2147	$4580	207
Professors	2762	4631	163. 6
Department heads in libraries	1090	2269	202. 2
Assistant professors	1740	2768	156. 8

Since Works, many writers have commented on salaries of librarians, but these studies have not generally made
explicit reference to such factors as educational attainment.
Heim and Cameron, for example, in 1970 maintained that:
(1) the salary range of librarians was too small; (2) the profession offered few high paying positions; and (3) faculty
members received higher salaries than librarians.

An imbalance between the compensations of faculty and librarians may well be symptomatic of two equally serious problems: minimization of the role and organizational requirements of this important facet of our educational-research program, and the possibility of exploitation. [43]

Heim and Cameron show that about 50% of the faculty members are in the two highest academic ranks, in contrast to about 50% of the librarians in the basic rank. Comparisons in this study are drawn between the traditional ranks for faculty members and administrative positions for librarians.[44]

Regrettably, Heim and Cameron say nothing about the comparative preparation of librarians and faculty members. This is of major importance. It should be noted that in the teaching profession the doctorate is related both to salary levels and to academic rank. The NEA Research Division in 1965-66 found that persons who had the doctorate upon being promoted to the rank of professor earned $588 more in public and $600 more in private institutions than those without that degree. The range of differences in salaries was from $300 to $2,500 more for those with the doctorate. For those with the rank of associate professor the median difference was $468; for assistant professors and for instructors it was $400. [45]

There is also a relationship between having the doctorate and academic rank and this relationship was greater in 1962-63 than it was in 1953-54 (see Table 11). [46] Furthermore, the median salary for professors, as is shown by the NEA report (see Table 12), was nearly double that for instructors. [47] Thus the person with the doctorate earns more

TABLE 11

Percentage of Faculty Members with the Doctorate in
Various Academic Ranks in American Colleges and
Universities in 1953-54 and 1962-63

Academic Rank	1953-54	1962-63
Professors	71	78
Associate Professors	46	61
Assistant Professors	30	42
Instructors	11	10

TABLE 12

Median Salaries of Faculty Members in 1, 017
Colleges and Universities in 1965-66

Professors	$12, 953
Associate Professors	10, 058
Assistant Professors	8, 417
Instructors	6, 761
All Ranks	9, 081

within any rank, and having the doctorate is also related to
promotion in rank.

To provide some indication of the salary similarities
or differences between faculty members and librarians,
averages were calculated for 1965-66 for the institutions
surveyed in the present study.   Eighteen of the colleges and
universities supplied salary information for the study by the
American Association of University Professors on faculty
salaries, and the nineteenth (Southwest Minnesota State College) was not yet in full operation at that time.   Unfortunately, the statistics published by the American Library Association did not include salary information for librarians at
Central Michigan University, Northern Michigan University,
St. Cloud State College, and Wisconsin State University at
Platteville.   Thus the comparisons are drawn between faculty
members and librarians at the 14 institutions for which
salary statistics are available for both groups.   Because of
the way in which the AAUP statistics were reported, [48] the
salaries for the faculty members represent an average of the
average salaries at the 14 institutions (see Table 13).   The
averages for the head librarians and the associate librarians
(an administrative position just below the director) were calculated separately, but all others were combined into one
group under the heading "all other librarians" (see Table 14).
If several librarians were listed in one group and if only low
and high salaries were given, mid-points were used in cal-
culating averages. [49]   Since information on the educational
background of the subjects was not available, no allowance
could be made for that factor, but all averages were com-
puted on a nine-month basis.   The results may be used as
a rough indication of conditions in 1965-66.   The average

TABLE 13

Average Salaries of Faculty Members in 1965-66 in
14 Institutions Included in
the Present Survey

Professors	$11,009
Associate Professors	9,330
Assistant Professors	8,440
Instructors	7,166

TABLE 14

Average Salaries of Librarians in 1965-66 in
14 Institutions Included in
the Present Survey

Head librarians	$11,209
Associate librarians	9,012
All other librarians	7,369

salary of the head librarians was slightly higher than that
for professors, but the earnings of the associate librarians
were below those of associate professors. The average for
all other librarians was above that for instructors but well
below that for assistant professors.

Tenure

Writing in 1967, Rockafellow defined tenure as "that
state of affairs under which a person holds and enjoys the
security of his employment." The term of appointment may
be for specified number of years, automatically renewed unless the employee is notified to the contrary, or permanent
after the completion of a probationary period. Tenure legislation normally stipulates procedures which apply to the con-
tinuation or termination of the incumbent in his position.

Concerned mainly with conditions in public schools,

Rockafellow found that the need for job security grew out of
the spoils system.   To counteract the evils of that system,
Civil Service was instituted for government employees.   For
teachers, tenure legislation reflected the need for protection
against capricious actions of boards of education and auto-
cratic administrators.

        In 1873 President Charles Eliot of Harvard spoke to
the National Education Association about the need for job
security to assure dignity for the teaching profession, and
in 1884 the NEA produced its first major statement which
called for legal protection against arbitrary dismissal. When
the American Federation of Teachers was founded in 1916,
it also took up the cause of job security. [50]

        In 1915, soon after the founding of the Association,
the Committee on Academic Freedom and Academic Tenure
of the AAUP formulated that Association's first statement on
academic freedom and tenure, the "1915 Declaration of Principles. "   This was officially approved by the membership of
the Association at its second annual meeting held in Washington, D. C. , on December 31, 1915, and January 1, 1916.
After a number of revisions the Association adopted the document which is known as the "1940 Statement of Principles
on Academic Freedom and Tenure. "[51] Since then, more
than 50 other professional groups have endorsed the statement. [52]

        After adapting it to fit libraries, the American Li-
brary Association adopted the statement on June 21, 1946.
This version is "A Statement of Principles of Intellectual
Freedom and Tenure for Librarians. "[53]

        A recent recommendation which extends the basic
principles embodied in the documents cited above deserves
a brief examination.   A special committee of the local chapter of the AAUP at Miami University maintained that tenure
alone was not enough.   The faculty member also needs assurance that he will be treated fairly in matters of salary,
research opportunities, teaching duties, and channels for re-
dress of grievances.   Any forces within the university which
create a sense of insecurity in the faculty member may
cause him, as a human being subject to the usual frailties,
to modify his views in order to make them more acceptable
to institutional pressures.   To insure an appropriate degree
of academic freedom, the faculty member needs unfettered
opportunity to advance in salary and rank, to engage in

research, and to participate in academic policy judgments.
If the faculty member cannot question existing theories, be-
liefs, and governing policies, society is the loser. As one
means of protecting the individual faculty member, the hierarchical structure must be kept to a minimal level essential for efficiency of operation. Competence and accomplishments of faculty members should be judged primarily by
colleagues rather than by the administrator. [54]

How can these concepts be applied to librarians?
Some library administrators believe the director should have
much latitude in personnel matters. Consequently the staff
member would have limited job security. Munthe, in his
book published in 1939, expressed amazement at the power
the American library administrator had over his staff. [55]
Hinting that it might be an undesirable trait, Farley, in his
1967 dissertation on the American library executive, found
directors of academic libraries to be more authoritarian and
aloof than their counterparts in public libraries. At the
same time he seemed to consider authoritarianism a virtue
in those who received their Ph. D. degrees from the Graduate Library School at the University of Chicago. [56]

According to David Weber, tenure pertains to librarians in a special way. It assures librarians of academic
freedom in book selection, disseminating information, and
advising library users; but the librarian should not be im-
mune to institutional pressures in policies relating to book
selection, planning buildings, circulation, and classification.
After quoting Fritz Machlup's 1964 statement that the major
justification for tenure is that it may encourage an insecure
person to express his views, Weber categorically states that
this has no application to librarians. He believes that the
librarian must be free from the threat of dismissal merely
because the administrator dislikes his subordinate's personality or opinions. Nevertheless, he suggests in his con-
cluding statement that the chief librarian should not be
hampered by tenure regulations which are as formalized as
those which apply to the professor.

Weber holds that the director should be able to terminate any librarian's appointment if the director judges the
individual to be a detriment to effective service. Since staff
relations are of crucial concern in a library, anyone who by
virture of personality characteristics causes conflict should
be subject to dismissal. The chief reasons for a tenure
policy, according to Weber, are its contributions to job

security, staff morale, recruiting, enchancing the librarian's
status, and improving the librarian-professor relationship. [57]

The Personnel Organization and Procedure: A Manual
Suggested for Use in College and University Libraries (here-
after referred to as the Manual), prepared by a special committee of the American Library Association, also tends to
place the employee's future at the whim of the immediate su-
pervisor and the director.   Evidently the librarian has no
contract under these guidelines, for the new employee can be
dismissed at a month's notice.   When terminations in cases
of "dismissal for incompetence, insubordination, or mental
or physical disability" affect staff members on "permanent
appointment, " the Manual suggests three months' notice. [58]

Thus the Manual supports David Weber's contention
that librarians should be treated differently from faculty members.   Furthermore, both the Manual and Weber probably
would concur with Robert Muller's view that the library is a
hierarchical organization whereas an academic department is
not. [59]   The Committee on Academic Status of the University
Libraries Section of the Association of College and Research
Libraries (ACRL) expressed a similar view when it stated
that the accomplishments of the librarian, and therefore his
salary and rank, "shall be evaluated by his superior officers
rather than by his colleagues. "[60]

Neither the Manual nor Weber would seem to put much
stock in the concept of grievance procedures and peer review
as enunciated in the 1969 ACRL resolution. [61]

The approach of the recent statement by Branscomb,
writing as a member of the Committee on Academic Status of
the University Libraries Section of ACRL, reflects quite a
different view.   Published in 1965, this document discussed
both the benefits and obligations of tenure and was emphatic
about the applicability of these principles to all members of
the professional staff on an equal basis.   Furthermore, rather
than drawing distinctions between practices for librarians and
the faculty, Branscomb, without specifically stating so, evidently worked on the assumption that procedures should be
identical for both groups and also urged the adoption of these
principles regardless of whether the librarians have or do not
have faculty status at a particular institution.

After commenting on the intellectual nature of library
tasks, he cited some of the activities which make it necessary

for the librarian to have the protection of academic freedom.
These pertain particularly to questions arising from the handling of controversial materials as the librarian encounters
them in selection, providing access, shelving locations, ex-
hibits, compiling bibliographies, planning library facilities,
publicizing library policies, publishing articles or giving
speeches, the use of possibly unorthodox cataloging and
classification procedures, experimenting with new methods of
library management or operation, and the advising of students.   The librarian, then, needs the protection of academic
freedom both in expressing his views and in performing his
duties. [62]

Williams maintained that the "greater the degree of
faculty control, the greater is likely to be the intellectual
superiority and distinction on the part of the whole university. "[63]   In 1962 Vosper wrote that the emphasis and reward
of only the administrative aspects of librarianship was inhibiting the intellectual development of the profession. [64]   At
least one major university library is attempting to make a
change.   David Kaser, Director of the Cornell University
Libraries, recently outlined a plan to make the library a
more democratic organization by shifting the management
responsibilities to the entire professional staff.

In recognition of the fact that there is something in-
herently inimical between the centralized determination
of production and service standards in traditionally hierarchical libraries and the rapidly increasingly professionalism of librarianship, we attempted during the year
to transfer as much as possible of library policy making
from the several management echelons to the 130 librarians themselves.   I know of no other library that has
gone as far as we have in this direction, so there is no
accepted pattern for us to follow.   Since there is much
in the training and responsibilities of librarians that is
similar to the training and responsibilities of teaching
faculty, we concluded that we might do well to adminis-
ter the work of our librarians as faculty work is ad-
ministered.   We are therefore restructuring our administrative procedures to parallel as far as possible those
of a college faculty and are moderately optimistic that
we are on the right track.   Thus far at least we have
encountered no unanticipated hurdles. [65]

Presumably, if libraries move away from the traditional hierarchical structure, a natural concomitant will be

greater participation by the entire staff in library planning
and management, and this was one objective of the ACRL resolution submitted to the ALA convention in 1969. [66]   And if
the librarian has a voice in library management, the concept
of tenure becomes all the more important.   As a professional who is interested in the effective development of his
organization, the librarian, as Blake pointed out in 1968,
may find himself espousing ideas concerning library management which may be in direct conflict with his administrator.
In such instances tenure serves the same purpose for librarians as it does for the faculty.

        Blake wrote that the academic librarian with tenure
was still the exception rather than the rule. [67]   However,
Downs in 1960 thought librarians were likely to receive more
favorable treatment in this regard than faculty members.
Because of the shortage of librarians, he maintained, administrators were likely to keep staff members even if they
were only performing at a minimally acceptable level. [68]
Stanford in 1964 reported a policy of exceptions (apparently
favoring librarians) at the University of Minnesota where librarians could gain tenure at the instructor's level and with
only the master's degree. [69]

Time and Funds for Publication and Research

        Because of the emphasis the academic community
places on scholarship, research and writing should be of
considerable concern to librarians.   Until recently few surveys have attempted to determine whether time or funds are
extended as inducements to encourage such activity.

        In 1968, all respondents among 72 directors of Ameri-
can Research Libraries and state universities said they favored research activity.   But the conclusions from comments
on the questionnaire were that assistance is often small, it
may be extended very selectively, and financial support
seems to be extended cautiously.   The sentiment that librarians should contribute substantially of their own time seemed
to predominate. [70]

        In Jesse and Mitchell's 1968 study, only one of 15 li-
brarians in liberal arts colleges gave an unqualified yes to
the question of whether a librarian could get time for research.   Among the universities, 15 respondents said they
allowed time and 16 said they did not.   All other respondents

gave qualified answers. However, one respondent stated that
he would certainly grant time if anyone should ask.   The
writers concluded that both the apathetic staff and reluctant
administrators share the blame for limited participation in
research activity. [71]

Although some writers have argued that scholarship
and the pursuit of truth must be accomplished regardless of
hours, [72] librarians have tended to plead exception because
of the necessity of maintaining rigid work schedules. [73]   Unlike the faculty member who can look forward to vacations
as a welcome respite of professional development through
broad reading, research, and writing, [74] and unlike the faculty member whose teaching load usually decreases as he
rises in rank, [75] the academic librarian, according to a 1969
survey, generally continues to be tied to the 40-hour week
and a month's vacation. [76]

Travel Funds

Paying expenses presumably encourages librarians to
attend conferences, but comparatively little has been written
specifically on this question.   On the basis of 78 replies
from state universities and land grant colleges and universities, Pope and Thompson reported in 1950 that 43 had a
separate budget for staff travel, but some of the others drew
on other sources.   Among those which had specified alloca-
tions the high was $1,325 and the low was $75, with a
median of $400.   In 59 instances all librarians were eligible
for travel funds, and in 39 institutions the entire staff qualified, but the sums available often necessitated the establish-
ment of various kinds of limitations.   Nevertheless, though
conditions were far from ideal and the practice of allowing
funds only for those in administrative positions existed in
some libraries, the respondents seemed to agree that librarians fared as well as faculty members with regard to
travel funds. [77]

In 1968 nearly all of Kellam and Barker's 72 respondents from members of the Association of Research Libraries
and other state universities said they paid expenses, and all
said they gave time for professional activities, yet only 78%
said they paid partial expenses for those who were not on
the program or were not members of committees.   The
writers added the lack of sufficient funds in many libraries
resulted in such practices as partial payment of expenses,

selectivity in authorizing travel, permitting travel on a ro-
tating basis, and giving priority to those who were on the
program or had committee meetings. [78]

   According to Elizabeth Stone's report, providing travel
funds is not of itself the critical factor in encouraging participation in professional activities.   If the administrator
wants his staff to attend conferences and institutes, the event
itself must be of high quality, and the staff member must
feel that he has a need to learn something which he can
apply to his job.   Thus Stone suggested that the librarian
who is given the opportunity to develop his full potential will
seek out those activities which will assist him in being a
success in his position regardless of availability or lack of
funds. [79]

Notes

1. W. E. Henry, "The Academic Standing of College Li-
    brary Assistants and Their Relation to the Carnegie
    Foundation, " Bulletin of the American Library Asso-
    ciation, 5 (July, 1911), 259-60.

2. George A. Works, College and University Library Prob-
    lems (Chicago: American Library Association, 1927),
    pp. 86-87.

3. James A. McMillen, "Academic Status of Library Staff
    Members of Large Universities, " CRL, 1 (March,
    1940), 140.

4. William M. Randall and Francis L. Goodrich, Princi-
    ples of College Library Administration (2nd ed. ;
    Chicago: American Library Association, 1941), pp.
    56-57.

5. John H. Moriarty, "Academic in Deed, " CRL, 31 (Jan-
    uary, 1970), 14-17.

6. See, for example, Tony B. Byles, "A Status Study of
    Teachers in Selected Colleges of Education in Louisi-
    ana" (unpublished Ed. D. dissertation, University of
    Southern Mississippi, 1963), p. 74.

7. Lloyd S. Woodburne, Principles of College and Univer-
    sity Administration (Stanford, Calif. : Stanford Uni-
    versity Press, 1958), pp. 68-70.

8. Mark H. Ingraham, The Mirror of Brass: The Compen-
    sation and Working Conditions of College and Univer-
    sity Administrators (Madison: University of Wisconsin
    Press, 1968), p. 261.

9. Carl Hintz, "Criteria for Appointment to and Promotion
    in Academic Rank," CRL, 29 (September, 1968),
    341-46.

10. University of Colorado Libraries, "Annual Report, 1967-
    1968," by Ralph E. Ellsworth (Boulder: University of
    Colorado Libraries, 1968), p. 4.

11. Walter C. Eells, "The Origin and Early History of
    Sabbatical Leave," AAUP Bulletin, 48 (Autumn, 1962),
    253-54.

12. Mark H. Ingraham, The Outer Fringe: Faculty Benefits
    Other than Annuities and Insurance (Madison: Univer-
    sity of Wisconsin Press, 1965), p. 76.

13. Ibid., p. 82.

14. Ibid., 72-82, 138.

15. U. S. Department of Health, Education, and Welfare,
    Office of Education, Sabbatical Leave in American
    Higher Education: Origin, Early History, and Current
    Practices, by Walter C. Eells and Ernest V. Hollis,
    Bulletin, 1962, No. 17 (Washington, D. C.: Govern-
    ment Printing Office, 1962), pp. 61-62.

16. "A Statement on Leaves of Absence," AAUP Bulletin,
    53 (Autumn, 1967), 270-74.

17. Ingraham, The Outer Fringe, pp. 73-75.

18. U. S. Department of Health, Education, and Welfare,
    Office of Education, Sabbatical Leave in American
    Higher Education, pp. 18, 44, 61-62.

19. Ingraham, The Mirror of Brass, pp. 86-90.

20. National Education Association, Research Division,
    Teacher Supply and Demand in Universities, Colleges,
    and Junior Colleges, 1959-60 and 1960-61, Research
    Report, 1961-R12 (Washington, D. C.: National Educa-
    tion Association, 1961), pp. 26-27.

21.   James Wright, "Fringe Benefits for Academic Library
      Personnel," CRL, 31 (January, 1970), 19-20.

22.   Vivian R. Boughter, "Salaries, Work Week, Vacations,
      Benefits, and Privileges of College Librarians,"
      CRL, 19 (March, 1958), 128.

23.   Raj Madan, Eliese Hetler, and Marilyn Strong, "The
      Status of Librarians in Four-Year State Colleges and
      Universities," CRL, 29 (September, 1968), 385.

24.   William H. Jesse and Ann E. Mitchell, "Professional
      Staff Opportunities for Study and Research," CRL, 29
      (March, 1968), 91-96.

25.   Ibid., p. 92.

26.   W. Porter Kellam and Dale L. Barker, "Activities and
      Opportunities of University Librarians for Full Parti-
      cipation in the Educational Enterprise," CRL, 29
      (May, 1968), 198.

27.   Sidney H. Ditzion, "College Librarians and the Higher
      Learning," in The Status of American College and
      University Librarians, ed. by Robert B. Downs,
      ACRL Monograph, No. 22 (Chicago: American Library
      Association, 1958), p. 157.

28.   Robert H. Muller, "Faculty Rank for Library Staff
      Members in Medium-Sized Universities and Colleges,"
      in The Status of American College and University
      Librarians, pp. 93-95.

29.   Guy R. Lyle, The Administration of the College Library
      (New York: H. W. Wilson Company, 1961), p. 196.

30.   William H. Carlson, College and University Libraries
      and Librarianship: An Examination of Their Present
      Status and Some Proposals for Their Future Develop-
      ment (Chicago: American Library Association, 1946),
      p. 83.

31.   Louis R. Wilson and Maurice F. Tauber, The Univer-
      sity Library (2nd ed.; New York: Columbia University
      Press, 1956), p. 297-98.

32.   Lyle, The Administration of the College Library, 1961,
      p. 183.

33. Ibid., pp. 194-95.

34. Kaspar D. Naegele and Elaine C. Stolar, "Income and Prestige," LJ, 85 (September 1, 1960), 2889.

35. Ibid., pp. 2888-90.

36. Rose Z. Sellers, "Statistics--the Earthy Approach," LJ, 80 (June 15, 1955), 1402-1404.

37. Harold D. Jones, "LACUNY: A Library Association in Action," California Librarian, 29 (July, 1968), 204-209.

38. Ingraham, The Mirror of Brass, pp. 81-82.

39. Robert L. Williams, The Administration of Academic Affairs in Higher Education (Ann Arbor: The University of Michigan Press, 1965), pp. 71-73.

40. Works, College and University Library Problems, pp. 88-89.

41. Ibid., p. 89.

42. Ibid., pp. 91-97.

43. Peggy Heim and Donald F. Cameron, The Economics of Librarianship in College and University Libraries, 1969-70: A Sample Survey of Compensations (Washington, D.C.: Council on Library Resources, Inc., 1970), p. 3.

44. Ibid., pp. 1-20.

45. "Financial Value of the Ph.D. for College Faculty Members," NEA Research Bulletin, 44 (October, 1966), 82-84.

46. Allan M. Cartter, "A New Look at the Supply of College Teachers," Educational Record, 46 (Summer, 1965), 275.

47. "Financial Value of the Ph.D. for College Faculty Members," p. 83.

48. "The Economic Status of the Profession: Report on the

Self-Grading Compensation Survey, 1965-66, " AAUP
Bulletin, 52 (Summer, 1966), 151, 175-76, 191.

49.   American Library Association, Library Administration
       Division, Library Statistics of Colleges and Universi-
       ties, 1965-66 Institutional Data (Chicago: American
       Library Association, 1967), pp. 190-95, 228-29.

50.   Theodore F. Rockafellow, "The Philosophy, Purpose,
       and Function of Tenure Legislation" (unpublished
       Ed. D. dissertation, Colorado State College, 1967),
       pp. 6-27.

51.   "Academic Freedom and Tenure: Statements of Princi-
       ples, " AAUP Bulletin, 42 (Spring, 1956), 41.

52.   "Academic Freedom and Tenure: 1940 Statement of
       Principles, " AAUP Bulletin, 53 (Summer, 1967), 246.

53.   "Tenure in Libraries: A Statement of Principles Adopted
       by the Council of the American Library Association,
       June 21, 1946, " ALA Bulletin, 40 (November, 1946),
       451-53.

54.   A Committee of the University of Miami Chapter of the
       AAUP, "Academic Freedom: Tenure Is Not Enough, "
       AAUP Bulletin, 53 (Summer, 1967), 202-209.

55.   Wilhelm Munthe, American Librarianship from a Euro-
       pean Angle (Chicago: American Library Association,
       1939), p. 162.

56.   Richard A. Farley, "The American Library Executive:
       An Inquiry into His Concepts of the Functions of His
       Office" (unpublished Ph. D. thesis, University of
       Illinois, 1967), pp. 76, 82.

57.   David C. Weber, "'Tenure' for Librarians in Academic
       Institutions, " CRL, 27 (March, 1966), 99-102.

58.   American Library Association, Personnel Publications
       Committee, Personnel Organization and Procedure: A
       Manual Suggested for Use in College and University
       Libraries (2nd ed. ; Chicago: American Library Asso-
       ciation, 1968), pp. 12, 16.

59.   Robert H. Muller, "Faculty Rank for Library Staff

Members in Medium-Sized Universities and Colleges,"
in The Status of American College and University Librarians, p. 91.

60.   Arthur M. McAnally, "Privileges and Obligations of
      Academic Status," CRL, 24 (March, 1963), 107-108.

61.   "Atlantic City Conference: A Great Show in Two Parts
      and a Cast of Thousands," ALA Bulletin, 63 (July-
      August, 1969), 952-53.

62.   Lewis C. Branscomb, "Tenure for Professional Li-
      brarians on Appointment at Colleges and Universities,"
      CRL, 26 (July, 1965), 297-98, 341.

63.   Robert L. Williams, The Administration of Academic
      Affairs in Higher Education (Ann Arbor: The Univer-
      sity of Michigan Press, 1965), p. 3.

64.   Robert Vosper, "Needed: An Open End Career Policy:
      A Critique of Classification and Pay Plans for Li-
      braries," ALA Bulletin, 56 (October, 1962), 833-35.

65.   Cornell University Libraries, "Report of the Director
      of the University Libraries, 1968-69," Ithaca, New
      York, 1969.   (Mimeographed.)

66.   "Atlantic City Conference: A Great Show in Two Parts
      and a Cast of Thousands," ALA Bulletin, 63 (July-
      August, 1969), 952-53.

67.   Fay M. Blake, "Tenure for the Academic Librarian,"
      CRL, 29 (November, 1968), 503-504.

68.   Robert B. Downs, "The Place of Librarians in Colleges
      and Universities," North Carolina Libraries, 18
      (Winter, 1960), 37.

69.   Edward B. Stanford, "Academic Status at Minnesota,"
      CRL, 25 (July, 1964), 260.

70.   Kellam and Barker, "Activities and Opportunities of
      University Librarians for Full Participation in the
      Educational Enterprise," pp. 196-97.

71.   Jesse and Mitchell, "Professional Staff Opportunities
      for Study and Research," pp. 89-90.

72. Russell H. Seibert, "Status and Responsibilities of
     Academic Librarians, " CRL, 22 (July, 1961), 253.

73. Jesse and Mitchell, "Professional Staff Opportunities
     for Study and Research, " p. 100.

74. Seibert, "Status and Responsibilities of Academic Li-
     brarians, " pp. 253-54.

75. Tony B. Byles, "A Status Study of Teachers in Se-
     lected Colleges of Education in Louisiana" (unpub-
     lished Ed. D. dissertation, University of Southern
     Mississippi, 1963), pp. 139-41.

76. Madan, Hetler, and Strong, "The Status of Librarians
     in Four-Year State Colleges and Universities, "
     pp. 385-86.

77. Mary F. Pope and Lawrence S. Thompson, "Travel
     Funds for University Library Staffs, " CRL, 11 (Jan-
     uary, 1950), 22-27.

78. Kellam and Barker, "Activities and Opportunities of
     University Librarians for Full Participation in the
     Educational Enterprise, " p. 198.

79. Elizabeth W. Stone, Factors Related to the Professional
     Development of Librarians (Metuchen, N. J. : Scare-
     crow Press, Inc. , 1969), pp. 200-213.

PART II

THE SURVEY

111

Chapter 5

General Characteristics of the Respondents

This chapter analyzes the characteristics of librarians and faculty members: their age, years of experience as professional librarians or college and university teachers, years at their present institutions, title of present positions, supervisory responsibilities (librarians only), teaching duties, and how librarians rank among ten groups of college and university personnel.

In certain instances more similarity exists between the male librarians and the male faculty members than between either the male and female librarians or the male and female faculty members. To some extent the differences by sex reflect divergence in career patterns which are generally consistent with those found in other studies, for many women tend to leave the labor force while their children are young.

The Sample

Because the faculty rosters published in college and university catalogs become outdated quickly, a personal letter was sent to the head librarians on October 1, 1969, requesting the names of the full-time professional librarians employed in the 19 institutions included in the survey. All head librarians responded; and on October 30, 1969, questionnaires were mailed to the 281 librarians whose names had been submitted. Usable responses were returned by 224 (79.9%) in time for analysis.

Either the regents' offices or officials supplied current rosters of faculty members at 13 colleges and universities. Obtaining the names for the other six institutions was more of a problem. Ultimately it became necessary to depend on college or university bulletins. Because faculty rosters in those publications were from one to two years old, it was to be expected that they would no longer be entirely accurate. Twelve faculty members originally selected for

the sample were thus excluded because they had moved to
other institutions, were part-time employees, or did not
qualify under the limitations established for the sample.
Possibly a few additional faculty members (from whom there
was no response) had moved or discarded the questionnaire.

The faculties at the 19 colleges and universities included 1, 754 individuals in the six departments chosen for
study: biology, economics, English, history, physics, and
sociology.   To get a sample which would produce results
roughly comparable in size to that for the librarians, questionnaires were sent to a random sample of 351 (20%) faculty
members.   Deducting the 12 who were later found to be outside of the guidelines for the survey left 339.

The cover letter and questionnaire for the faculty
were mailed on November 12, 1969.   Of the 339 subjects, 205
(60. 5%) returned usable replies in time to be analyzed.

Because they generally have considerable interest in
the question of faculty status, a comparatively high rate of
response was expected from the librarians, and the 79. 9%
return was no surprise.   Because they have less direct concern with this issue, the 60. 5% return from the faculty was
considered satisfactory.

The total sample then consists of 429, of whom 224
(52. 2%) are librarians and 205 (47. 8%) are faculty members.
Among the faculty, 162 (79%) are men and 43 (21%) are women.   Among the librarians, just over half, 113 (50. 4%), are
men and 111 (49. 6%) are women.

Age

The age of the librarians and faculty members is
shown in Tables 15 and 16.   Among the librarians the average age is 40. 9 years; for the men it is 39. 8, and for the
women 42. 1.   The average age of the faculty members is
39. 8; for the men it is 40. 4, and for the women 37. 6.   More
than one of every four librarians and one of every five faculty members is 30 years of age or younger.   Differences
between the percentages for men and women are sometimes
larger than those between male librarians and male faculty
members.   A larger percentage of female librarians and
faculty members is in the 25 to 30-year age span than in any
other.   For the male librarians the mode is 31 to 35, and

TABLE 15

Age of Librarians by Sex

Age	Men		Women		Total	
	No.	%	No.	%	No.	%
Under 25	1	. 9	13	11. 7	14	6. 3
25-30	22	19. 6	22	19. 8	44	19. 6
31-35	25	22. 3	15	13. 6	40	17. 8
36-40	18	16. 1	4	3. 6	22	9. 8
41-45	15	12. 5	6	5. 4	21	9. 4
46-50	17	15. 2	9	8. 1	26	11. 6
51-55	7	6. 2	21	18. 9	28	12. 5
56-60	6	5. 4	9	8. 1	15	6. 7
61-65	1	. 9	11	9. 9	12	5. 4
Over 65	1	. 9	1	. 9	2	. 9
Total	113	100. 0	111	100. 0	224	100. 0

TABLE 16

Age of Faculty Members by Sex

Age	Men		Women		Total	
	No.	%	No.	%	No.	%
Under 25	0		1	2. 3	1	. 5
25-30	25	15. 4	16	37. 4	41	20. 0
31-35	34	21. 0	5	11. 6	39	19. 0
36-40	40	24. 7	6	14. 0	46	22. 4
41-45	19	11. 7	6	14. 0	25	12. 2
46-50	21	13. 0	3	6. 9	24	11. 7
51-55	10	6. 2	3	6. 9	13	6. 3
56-60	9	5. 6	2	4. 7	11	5. 4
61-65	3	1. 8	1	2. 3	4	2. 0
Over 65	1	. 6	0	0. 0	1	. 5
Total	162	100. 0	43	100. 0	205	100. 0

for the male faculty members it is 36 to 40.

Of the female librarians 35 (31. 5%) are 30 years of age or younger, compared with 23 (20. 5%) of the male librarians and 25 (15. 4%) of the male faculty members. On the other hand more of the female librarians are aged 51 or older--42 (37. 8%), compared with 15 (13. 4%) of the male librarians and 23 (14. 2%) of the male faculty members. Nearly 40% of the female faculty members are 30 or younger.

Although the male librarians are on the average slightly younger, their distribution in the various age groupings is generally similar to that of the faculty men.

Years of Experience

A large percentage of both the librarians and the faculty members are newcomers to the academic world (see Tables 17 and 18).   The average number of years of experience for the librarians is 10. 4 years, 9. 3 for the men and 11. 5 for the women.   The faculty members have been college teachers for an average of 9. 6 years, 10. 5 for the men and 6. 6 for the women.   Nearly 40% of the librarians and more than 57% of the faculty members have had from three to ten years of experience.

Although their average length of experience is slightly longer than that of the faculty men or the male librarians, a large proportion of the female librarians are beginners.   In their first position as academic librarians, 14. 4% have under one year of experience.   Another 15. 3% have had from one to two years of experience and 16. 2% have had from three to five years.   Thus, 45. 9% began work within the past year or have had experience ranging up to five years.

The men are more evenly distributed in the various groupings; and while the academic librarians on the average have had slightly less experience, they are generally similar to the male faculty members.   Of the female faculty members 60. 5% have had from less than one to five years of experience.

Years at Present Institution

Tables 19 and 20 indicate the number of years the

TABLE 17

Years of Experience as Librarians by Sex

Years of Experience	Men		Women		Total	
	No.	%	No.	%	No.	%
Under 1	8	7. 1	16	14. 4	24	10. 7
1-2	15	13. 3	17	15. 3	32	14. 3
3-5	28	24. 8	18	16. 2	46	20. 5
6-10	27	23. 9	16	14. 4	43	19. 2
11-15	15	13. 3	9	8. 1	24	10. 7
16-20	12	10. 6	11	9. 9	23	10. 3
21-30	5	4. 4	17	15. 3	22	9. 8
Over 30	3	2. 6	7	6. 4	10	4. 5
Total	113	100. 0	111	100. 0	224	100. 0

TABLE 18

Years of Experience as College Teachers of Faculty Members by Sex

Years of Experience	Men		Women		Total	
	No.	%	No.	%	No.	%
Under 1	3	1. 9	1	2. 3	4	2. 0
1-2	15	9. 3	7	16. 3	22	10. 7
3-5	41	25. 3	18	41. 9	59	28. 8
6-10	46	28. 3	12	27. 9	58	28. 4
11-15	28	17. 3	3	7. 0	31	15. 1
16-20	12	7. 4	1	2. 3	13	6. 3
21-30	12	7. 4	1	2. 3	13	6. 3
Over 30	5	3. 1	0	0. 0	5	2. 4
Total	162	100. 0	43	100. 0	205	100. 0

respondents have been at their present institution. The
average librarian has been at his college or university for
5.6 years, the men for 4.9 and the women for 6.4. The
average faculty member has been at his institution for six
years, the men for 6.4 years and the women for 4.3 years.

Well over half of the respondents have been at their
present college or university for five years or fewer. This
holds true for 73 (65.8%) of the female librarians, 90 (79.7%)
of the male librarians, 107 (66.1%) of the male faculty members, and 36 (83.7%) of the female faculty members. Only
25 of the 429 respondents have been at their institution for
more than 15 years: nine (5.5%) of the male faculty members, six (5.3%) of the male librarians, and ten (9%) of the
female librarians.

More than one of every five librarians (22.8%) has
been at his institution less than one year, but this is true
for only approximately one of every 20 faculty members
(5.4%). The results of the questionnaire provide no answer
to this phenomenon. However, speculation might suggest
either that the libraries had a large staff turnover during
the past year or that the large percentage of new staff members resulted from a rapid growth in the libraries and the
consequent addition of new positions. If the percentage of
librarians who have been at their institution for less than a
year stems from internal expansion, then the libraries would
seem to be growing more rapidly than the colleges and universities themselves.

Position of Respondents

The questionnaire asked all respondents to give the
title of their position. Although 13 of the 205 faculty members have some administrative responsibilities such as chairman of a department, all of them teach and are alike at least
in that respect. Consequently the analysis here will be
limited to librarians.

The survey included 19 head librarians, of whom 17
responded. Of these, 14 are men and three are women.
Whereas nine of the 14 men have been chief librarians at
their present institution for fewer than five years, the three
women have all been at theirs for more than ten years.

Further analysis of the librarians by their positions

TABLE 19

Average Number of Years Librarians Have Been
at Their Present Institutions

Years at Institution	Men		Women		Total	
	No.	%	No.	%	No.	%
Under 1	22	19. 5	29	26. 1	51	22. 8
1-2	28	24. 8	24	21. 6	52	23. 2
3-5	40	35. 4	20	18. 1	60	26. 8
6-10	9	7. 9	16	14. 4	25	11. 2
11-15	8	7. 1	12	10. 8	20	8. 9
16-20	5	4. 4	2	1. 8	7	3. 1
21-30	1	. 9	7	6. 3	8	3. 5
Over 30	0	0. 0	1	. 9	1	. 5
Total	113	100. 0	111	100. 0	224	100. 0

TABLE 20

Average Number of Years Faculty Members Have Been
at Their Present Institutions

Years at Institution	Men		Women		Total	
	No.	%	No.	%	No.	%
Under 1	9	5. 6	2	4. 7	11	5. 4
1-2	39	24. 1	15	34. 8	54	26. 3
3-5	59	36. 4	19	44. 2	78	38. 1
6-10	34	21. 0	5	11. 6	39	19. 0
11-15	12	7. 4	2	4. 7	14	6. 8
16-20	1	. 6	0	0. 0	1	. 5
21-30	6	3. 7	0	0. 0	6	2. 9
Over 30	2	1. 2	0	0. 0	2	1. 0
Total	162	100. 0	43	100. 0	205	100. 0

must proceed with caution, for no precise terminology exists. If the chief administrator designates his position as head librarian, chief librarian, or director of libraries, the meaning is clear; but the title "librarian" may mean the director or any professional member of the staff. Associate librarian normally means that the person is in an administrative position just below the director. However, "assistant librarian" may mean essentially the same thing, or it may mean that the person is one among all the "assistant librarians" who constitute the staff. Similarly "reference librarian" may mean the head of the department or a librarian who works in that department. In spite of the fact that the meanings of titles vary from library to library, an effort was made to categorize the respondents by type of position held (see Table 21). The results may be suggestive, but no claim that they are entirely accurate is intended.

TABLE 21

Positions of Librarians by Sex

	Men		Women		Total	
	No.	%	No.	%	No.	%
Head Librarian	14	12.4	3	2.7	17	7.6
Associate librarian	5	4.4	1	.9	6	2.7
Heads of service (cataloging, reference, etc.)	33	29.2	24	21.6	57	25.4
Teaching	6	5.3	2	1.8	8	3.6
Non-administrative	48	42.5	72	64.9	120	53.6
Librarians[a]	7	6.2	9	8.1	16	7.1
Total	113	100.0	111	100.0	224	100.0

[a]These 16 simply listed their position in some general way such as "librarian."

At the two top administrative levels, that is, the head librarian and associate librarian, men clearly dominate. Male directors outnumber female directors by nearly five to

one and male associate librarians outnumber females by five
to one.   Below this level the results are not as precise.
Nevertheless, Table 21 tends to support the claim that men
are more likely to be in administrative positions than are
women.   Among the women, 64. 9% fall into the non-admin-
istrative group, as compared with 42. 5% of the men.

Supervisory Responsibilities

        The librarians were asked to indicate the number of
staff members they supervised.   If men seem to be more
likely to hold the administrative positions, one would then
also expect that they would hold more of the supervisory positions.   According to the results of this survey, that is indeed the case.   However, it is impossible to establish a
strict relationship between administrative and supervisory
positions; for a cataloger, for example, may supervise
several other employees without being head of that department.

        Men are more likely to be in those positions which
involve supervision (see Table 22).   Nearly 20% more women do not supervise any other librarians, and 21. 8% of the
men as compared with 6. 3% of the women supervise six or
more.   These figures, of course, result to some extent
from the fact that 14 of the 17 head librarians are men.

        Nearly three of every four (72. 3%) of the librarians
reported that they supervised supporting staff (see Table 23).
Women predominate in the non-supervisory group by 33. 3%
to 21. 1%, and in the group supervising from one to five by
55% to 48. 7%.   At the higher level, 29. 2% of the men as
compared with 11. 7% of the women supervise six or more.

How Librarians Rank Among Ten Academic Positions

        Although not intended as a sophisticated measure of
the status of librarians, one item on the questionnaire asked
faculty members and librarians to rank ten academic positions including librarians and faculty members in order of
importance from 1 (most) to 10 (least).   Because they may
have considered the very thought of differing levels of prestige in the academic community as a divisive element, 21
faculty members failed to complete this item; and several of
them explicitly stated that they considered this a question

TABLE 22

Supervision of Professional Staff by
Librarians by Sex

Number Supervised	Men		Women		Total	
	No.	%	No.	%	No.	%
None	56	49. 6	77	69. 4	133	59. 3
1-2	18	16. 1	20	18. 0	38	17. 0
3-5	14	12. 5	7	6. 3	21	9. 4
6-9	9	8. 0	4	3. 6	13	5. 8
10 or more	16	13. 8	3	2. 7	19	8. 5
Total	113	100. 0	111	100. 0	224	100. 0

TABLE 23

Supervision of Non-Professional Staff
by Librarians by Sex

Number Supervised	Men		Women		Total	
	No.	%	No.	%	No.	%
None	25	22. 1	37	33. 3	62	27. 7
1-2	42	37. 2	42	37. 9	84	37. 5
3-5	13	11. 5	19	17. 1	32	14. 3
6-9	11	9. 7	6	5. 4	17	7. 6
10 or more	22	19. 5	7	6. 3	29	12. 9
Total	113	100. 0	111	100. 0	224	100. 0

TABLE 24

Median Rankings of Ten Positions from 1 (Most) to
10 (Least Important) by Faculty Members by Sex

	Men	Women	Total
Academic dean	2	1	1
Faculty (Arts and Sciences)	1	2	2
Education faculty	3	4	3
Librarians	4	4	4
Dean of men and women	5	5	5
Admissions officer	6	5	6
Business officer	7	6	7
Counselors	7	7	7
Media specialists	7	8	7
Coaches	9	10	9

TABLE 25

How Librarians Think Faculty Would Rank Ten Positions
by Sex--Median Rankings from 1 (Most) to 10 (Least Important)

	Men	Women	Total
Academic dean	1	1	1
Faculty (Arts and Sciences)	2	2	2
Education faculty	3	3	3
Dean of men and women	4	4	4
Admissions officer	5	5	5
Business officer	6	7	6
Librarians	6	7	7
Media specialists	7	8	7
Coaches	8	7	8
Counselors	9	9	9

which should not be broached.   For essentially the same reason, or pleading lack of acquaintance with the faculty, 43 librarians refused to respond to the question asking them how they thought the faculty at their institution would rank librarians.   Finally, 34 librarians did not wish to commit themselves on how librarians should rank among the ten positions.   Table 24 is therefore based on 184 replies (143 men, 41 women), Table 25 on 181 (94 men and 87 women), and Table 26 on 190 (96 men and 94 women).

Some librarians believe the faculty holds librarians in low esteem, and the most noteworthy result of this item is that the librarians fare better than they thought they would. Although the librarians thought the faculty would place them in the number 7 position, faculty members actually ranked them in 4, below only the college of arts and sciences faculty, the academic dean, and the education faculty.   This is the same relative position which librarians believe they should hold.

TABLE 26

Median Rankings of Ten Positions from 1 (Most) to
10 (Least Important) by Librarians by Sex

	Men	Women	Total
Academic dean	1	1	1
Faculty (Arts and Sciences)	2	2	2
Education faculty	3	3	3
Librarians	3	4	4
Dean of men and women	5	5	5
Media specialists	5	6	5
Admissions officer	7	7	7
Counselors	7	7	7
Business officer	8	8	8
Coaches	9	9	9

In spite of the fact that several librarians stated that librarians and media specialists were identical, the librarians ranked themselves fourth and the other group fifth; but while faculty members ranked librarians fourth, they placed the instructional media specialists in seventh position.

Interestingly, the male librarians think the faculty would rank them in the number 6 position but actually rank themselves in number 3, but the female librarians think the faculty would rank librarians seventh and actually rank themselves fourth.

According to the results of the present survey librarians enjoy more prestige in the academic community than they think they do. Thus some of the concern on the part of librarians about status, in the sense of acceptance by the academic community, seems unwarranted. A complicating factor may be the possibility that librarians are more highly esteemed by the faculty than they are by the administrative officials, which could create frustration for the librarians in their dealings with the central administration, but this is a matter of speculation which might be worthy of further investigation.

Teaching

The majority of librarians, 168 (75%), are not engaged in classroom teaching. Forty-four (19. 6%) of the librarians teach an average of 3. 1 hours per week, and another 12 (5. 4%) teach an average of 8. 8 hours (see Table 27). Probably the major portion of the time of the 12 is devoted to duties not directly related to library service, but they were included in the survey because the head librarians submitted their names as members of the library staff. Possibly the teaching duties of these individuals may vary from term to term.

More women than men spend time in the classroom, 33 of the former as compared with 23 of the latter. The women teach an average of 4. 5 hours whereas the men teach an average of 4. 2 hours.

Among the faculty the average teaching load is 11 for the men and 12. 4 for the women (see Table 28). By rank, the 115 instructors and assistant professors teach an average of 11. 7 hours and the 90 associate and full professors 10. 8 hours. For all ranks the average is 11. 3 hours, and the mode is 12 hours.

TABLE 27

Average Number of Hours Taught by Librarians

	Number of Individuals	Average Number of Hours Per Week
Do not teach	168	0
Teach 1-6 hours	44	3. 1
Teach 7-12 hours	12	8. 8
Men who teach	23	4. 2
Women who teach	33	4. 5

TABLE 28

Average Number of Hours Taught by
Faculty Members by Rank and Sex

	Number of Hours
Instructors and assistant professors	11. 7
Associate professors and professors	10. 8
Men	11. 0
Women	12. 4
Total	11. 3

Chapter 6

Problems and Responsibilities of Faculty Status

This chapter analyzes the responses regarding (1) education, (2) publication and research, (3) participation in faculty government, (4) professional activities, and (5) sex. Of these, education and research and publication are the most critical. Because differences by sex are discussed throughout the survey, that facet will be treated as a summary statement rather than a detailed analysis.

Education

Various writers have expressed the view either that librarians already have attained an impressive level of education or, the opposing view, that librarians need much additional graduate work in order to meet faculty standards. The present survey supports the evidence from previous studies indicating that the educational level of librarians is rising.

Highest Degrees of Librarians

Nearly all of the librarians, 216 (96. 4%), in the 19 state colleges and universities have at least the master's degree (see Table 29). While 141 (62. 9%) have the master's in library science as the highest degree, another 13 (5. 8%) have the sixth-year degree, and 50 (22. 3%) have two master's degrees. Eight (3. 6%) hold only the bachelor's degree. At the same time only a small number, 12 (5. 4%), have the doctorate.

That librarians are pursuing graduate study beyond their highest degree is indicated by the fact that 143, or nearly two-thirds of them, have done so. A total of 101 (45. 1%) have earned from one to 30 credits, another 33 (14. 7%) have earned from 31 to 60 credits, and nine (4%) have earned more than 60 credits. The men have earned an average of 22. 3 semester credits, the women 10. 1. The total average is 16. 1. Of the librarians, 71 (31. 7%) expect

TABLE 29

Highest Degrees Held by Librarians by Sex

	Men		Women		Total	
	No.	%	No.	%	No.	%
Bachelor's	2	1. 8	6	5. 4	8	3. 6
Master's[a]	65	57. 5	76	68. 5	141	62. 9
Two master's[b]	33	29. 2	17	15. 3	50	22. 3
Sixth-year degree[c]	4	3. 5	9	8. 1	13	5. 8
Doctorate[d]	9	8. 0	3	2. 7	12	5. 4
Total[e]	113	100. 0	111	100. 0	224	100. 0

[a]Ten of these have a master's degree in a subject other than library science, mainly in educational media, and nine have the older fifth-year bachelor's degree which for the purposes of discussion is considered the equivalent of the fifth-year master's degree in library science.

[b]Six of these have the older fifth-year bachelor's degree in library science which for the purposes of discussion is considered the equivalent of the fifth-year master's degree.

[c]Of the 13, nine have the sixth-year certificate and four have the older sixth-year master's degree. The two degrees are combined under the "sixth-year degree."

[d]Three of these are the Ed. D. and nine are the Ph. D.

[e]Of the total sample 11 (4. 9%) reported no background in library science.

to earn another degree (see Table 30). Naturally many contingencies will affect what happens in this area. Should all those who are now employed in the 19 institutions under study receive their degrees according to current plans, one could predict that, within the next five to ten years, 42 (18. 8%) would have the doctorate, and another group of perhaps 86 (38. 4%) would have two master's degrees. In addition, 18

(8%) would have the sixth-year specialist certificate.   Some
146 (65. 2%) of these librarians, then, would have the doctorate, a master's in addition to the basic professional degree,
or a sixth-year certificate.   These figures do not include the
20 (8. 9%) who were undecided; most of these expressed a
desire to continue their education at some time if it became
feasible. (The percentages in the text are based on the total
sample of 224 respondents.   Those in Table 30 are based on
212.)

TABLE 30

Advanced Degrees Expected by Librarians by Sex

	Men		Women		Total	
	No.	%	No.	%	No.	%
None	55	52. 9	66	61. 0	121	57. 1
Second master's	15	14. 4	21	19. 4	36	16. 9
Sixth-year degree	3	2. 9	2	1. 9	5	2. 4
Doctorate[a]	19	18. 3	11	10. 2	30	14. 2
Undecided	12	11. 5	8	7. 5	20	9. 4
Total[b]	104	100. 0	108	100. 0	212	100. 0

[a]Five of these are the Ed. D. degree.

[b]The 12 who already have the doctorate are excluded
from the table.

Of the librarians with the doctorate in the present
survey, three are directors, two are assistant directors,
one is head of technical services, two are working and teaching in the area of instructional media, one is a government
documents librarian, one is a cataloger, one is an acquisi-
tion librarian, and one is the head of a curriculum library.
Thus eight of the 12 are major executives or involved with
teaching.   The remaining four would seem to have minor
administrative responsibilities, although titles such as catalog or acquisitions librarian may mean either that the person
directs the department or is simply working in that area.

As a group the head librarians have a higher level of

TABLE 31

Education of Head Librarians in 17 Institutions

	Men		Women		Total	
	No.	%	No.	%	No.	%
M. A. in L. S.	3	21. 4	1	33. 3	4	23. 6
Two master's	8	57. 2	1	33. 3	9	52. 9
Sixth-year degree	0	0. 0	1	33. 3	1	5. 9
Doctorate	3	21. 4	0	0. 0	3	17. 6
Total	14	100. 0	3	100. 0	17	100. 0

education than the average for the total sample of librarians. Table 31 shows that 17. 6% have the doctorate, just over half (52. 9%) have two master's degrees, 5. 9% have the sixth-year degree. While 33. 5% of the total sample of librarians have graduate degrees beyond the fifth-year master's, 76. 4% of the directors have that much education. Nevertheless, that the doctorate is not required for the position of head librarian is shown by the fact that only three of the 17 have that degree.

Highest Degrees of Faculty Members

When comparisons are made with the faculty, fewer librarians on the average have undertaken formal study beyond the master's degree and fewer librarians have the doctorate. For the faculty the degree itself is an important factor in promotion. As shown in the section on academic rank (see Chapter 7), 100% of the faculty members who are professors have the doctorate, as do 84% of the associate professors, 46% of the assistant professors, and 2. 6% of the instructors.

Over half (57. 6%) of the faculty respondents have the doctorate (see Table 32). With one exception, all the rest have the master's degree. One should add to these figures those for formal study beyond their highest degree as well as expectations for the master's and doctorate (see Table 33).

The average number of semester credits earned by

TABLE 32

Highest Degrees of Faculty Members by Sex

	Men		Women		Total	
	No.	%	No.	%	No.	%
Bachelor's		0. 0	1	2. 3	1	. 5
Master's	56	34. 6	30	69. 8	86	41. 9
Doctorate[a]	106	65. 4	12	27. 9	118	57. 6
Total	162	100. 0	43	100. 0	205	100. 0

[a]Of these three have the Ed. D. degree.

TABLE 33

Average Number of Credits Beyond
Highest Degree Earned by Faculty Members

	No. of Faculty[a]	Average No. of Semester Credits
Men	56	36. 2
Women	31	21. 0
Total	87	30. 9

[a]The 106 men and 12 women who have the doctorate
are excluded from the table.

the faculty members who do not have the doctorate is 30. 9.
This is roughly equivalent to the requirement for the master's degree in many universities, but the men have earned
an average of 15. 2 hours more than have the women.

Table 34 shows the percentage of faculty members
who expect to earn another degree. Adding those who anticipate earning the doctorate to those who already have it

brings this total to 181 (88. 3%).   Of those who do not have
the doctorate, 78. 8% hope to complete that degree within the
next five years.

TABLE 34

Advanced Degrees Expected by Faculty Members by Sex

	Men		Women		Total	
	No.	%	No.	%	No.	%
None	11	19. 6	11	35. 5	22	25. 3
Master's	0	0. 0	0	0. 0	0	0. 0
Doctorate[a]	45	80. 4	18	58. 0	63	72. 4
Undecided	0	0. 0	2	6. 5	2	2. 3
Total	56	100. 0	31	100. 0	87	100. 0

[a]The 106 men and 12 women who have the doctorate
are excluded from the table.

Pressure to Work Toward the Doctorate

Naturally many faculty members and librarians work
toward advanced degrees because they feel compelled by institutional pressures, professional expectations, or personal
aspirations.   Because of this, one item on the questionnaire
asked whether the respondent felt that he or she was under
pressure to work toward the doctorate.

As one might expect, faculty members feel (or felt
before they earned the degree) that they are under greater
pressure to earn the doctorate than do librarians (see
Tables 35 and 36).   Nearly three times the percentage of librarians feel under no pressure, 143 (63. 8%) as compared
with 44 (21. 5%) of the faculty.

Although the female faculty members felt less pressure to work toward the doctorate than do the faculty men,
the difference between the male and female faculty members
is less than that between the female faculty members and
the male librarians.   Furthermore, the difference between

TABLE 35

Pressure to Work Toward the Doctorate
by Librarians by Sex

	Men		Women		Total	
	No.	%	No.	%	No.	%
Strong pressure	14	12. 4	3	2. 7	17	7. 6
Mild pressure	35	30. 9	21	18. 9	56	25. 0
No pressure	62	54. 9	81	73. 0	143	63. 8
No response	2	1. 8	6	5. 4	8	3. 6
Total	113	100. 0	111	100. 0	224	100. 0

TABLE 36

Pressure to Work Toward the Doctorate
by Faculty Members by Sex

	Men		Women		Total	
	No.	%	No.	%	No.	%
Strong pressure	81	50. 0	20	46. 5	101	49. 2
Mild pressure	41	25. 3	9	20. 9	50	24. 4
No pressure	31	19. 1	13	30. 3	44	21. 5
No response	9	5. 6	1	2. 3	10	4. 9
Total	162	100. 0	43	100. 0	205	100. 0

the male and female librarians is considerable. The
female librarians feel least pressure.   Only 2. 7% of
them feel strong pressure, in comparison with 50% of
the male faculty members, 46. 5% of the female faculty
members, and 12. 4% of the male librarians.   At the
other extreme, 73% of the female librarians feel no
pressure, followed by 54. 9% of the male librarians and
30. 3% of the female and 19. 1% of the male faculty members.

A few librarians stated that they felt no pressure to work toward the doctorate but then added that they would not be eligible for promotion to associate or full professor without that degree.   Consequently the institution itself in some instances is providing an inducement to further education.

Librarians who are 35 years of age or younger account for 43. 7% of the total librarian sample, but they represent 61. 1% of all those who anticipate earning another master's and 72% of those who anticipate earning the doctorate.   Furthermore, this same group includes 64. 7% of the 17 who feel strong pressure to work toward the doctorate and 44. 7% of the 56 who feel mild pressure.   Thus the younger group seems to feel a greater compulsion to work toward advanced degrees.

Recommendations for Minimal and Terminal Degrees for Librarians

One more point needs to be considered--the librarians' and faculty members' suggestions for minimal and terminal education for librarians.   Both among the librarians (69. 2%) and faculty members (53. 7%) the largest percentage recommended the master's degree in library science as the minimal level of education (see Tables 37 and 38).   Approximately the same percentage of male (69. 1%) and female (69. 4%) librarians considered this the appropriate preparation, and more of the faculty women (65. 1%) concurred than did faculty men (50. 6%).

More faculty men (25. 9%) than any other single group suggested the bachelor's degree in library science as the first professional degree; of the librarians, 12. 6% of the women and 8. 8% of the men would agree.   Support for degrees other than the master's or the bachelor's in library science was comparatively small.   In proposing the bachelor's as a first degree faculty members may be recommending a policy consistent with practices in other disciplines. Some departments in state colleges accept teachers with the bachelor's degree as part-time instructors on a temporary basis while the individual is working toward an advanced degree.

For the terminal degrees about half of the faculty members (50. 2%) deemed the doctorate to be the most appropriate degree and 19. 6% of the librarians would agree (see Tables 39 and 40).   A significant proportion of librarians (cont. p. 138)

TABLE 37

Librarians' Recommendations for Minimal Degrees
for Librarians by Sex

	Men		Women		Total	
	No.	%	No.	%	No.	%
Bachelor's in library science	10	8.8	14	12.6	24	10.7
Bachelor's in other subject	5	4.4	5	4.5	10	4.4
Master's in library science	78	69.1	77	69.4	155	69.2
Master's in other subject	4	3.5	2	1.8	6	2.7
Master's in library science plus subject master's	10	8.8	9	8.1	19	8.5
Doctorate in library science	1	.9	0	0.0	1	.5
Qualified response[a]	3	2.7	3	2.7	6	2.7
No response	2	1.8	1	.9	3	1.3
Total	113	100.0	111	100.0	224	100.0

[a]Some respondents qualified their answer by stating
that depending upon the position he holds, the librarian may
need a master's, two master's degrees, a doctorate in
library science, or a doctorate in another subject area.

TABLE 38

Faculty Recommendations for Minimal Degrees
for Librarians by Sex

	Men		Women		Total	
	No.	%	No.	%	No.	%
Bachelor's in library science	42	25. 9	7	16. 3	49	23. 9
Bachelor's in other subject	5	3. 1	2	4. 7	7	3. 4
Master's in library science	82	50. 6	28	65. 1	110	53. 7
Master's in other subject	6	3. 7	1	2. 3	7	3. 4
Master's in library science plus subject master's	6	3. 7	2	4. 7	8	3. 9
Doctorate	0	0. 0	1	2. 3	1	0. 5
Qualified response[a]	14	8. 6	1	2. 3	15	7. 3
No response	7	4. 4	1	2. 3	8	3. 9
Total	162	100. 0	43	100. 0	205	100. 0

[a]Some respondents qualified their answers by stating
that depending upon the position he holds, the librarian may
need a master's, two master's degrees, the doctorate in
library science, or the doctorate in another subject area.

TABLE 39

Librarians' Recommendations for Terminal Degrees
for Librarians by Sex

	Men		Women		Total	
	No.	%	No.	%	No.	%
Bachelor's in library science	2	1. 8	0	0. 0	2	0. 9
Master's in library science	37	32. 6	30	27. 0	67	29. 9
Master's in other subject	3	2. 7	2	1. 8	5	2. 2
Master's in library science plus subject master's	23	20. 4	33	29. 7	56	25. 0
Doctorate[a]	24	21. 2	20	18. 0	44	19. 6
Qualified response[b]	20	17. 7	17	15. 3	37	16. 5
No response	4	3. 6	9	8. 2	13	5. 9
Total	113	100. 0	111	100. 0	223	100. 0

[a]Includes one Ed. D. and 14 Ph. D. 's in subject areas other than library science.

[b]Depending upon the position he holds, the librarian may need the master's, two master's degrees, the doctorate in library science, or a doctorate in another subject area.

TABLE 40

Faculty Recommendations for Terminal Degrees
for Librarians by Sex

	Men		Women		Total	
	No.	%	No.	%	No.	%
Bachelor's in library science	1	0.6	0	0.0	1	0.5
Bachelor's in other subject	0	0.0	0	0.0	0	0.0
Master's in library science	28	17.3	9	20.9	37	18.1
Master's in other subject	5	3.1	0	0.0	5	2.4
Master's in library science plus subject master's	9	5.6	2	4.7	11	5.4
Doctorate[a]	79	48.8	24	55.8	103	50.2
Qualified response[b]	31	19.1	6	14.0	37	18.1
No response	9	5.5	2	4.6	11	5.3
Total	162	100.0	43	100.0	205	100.0

[a]Included 84 recommendations for the doctorate in library science, 17 for a degree in subject areas other than library science and two for the Ed. D. degree.

[b]Depending upon the position he holds the librarian may need a master's, two master's degrees, the doctorate in library science, or a doctorate in another subject area.

(25%) believe the second master's degree is of greater value
than the doctorate, and 29. 9% would settle for the master's
in library science.   While few of the faculty members (5. 4%)
seem to place value on the second master's, many of them
(18. 1%) agree that the master's in library science is sufficient.   Approximately one-third of the librarians and one-
fifth of the faculty members set the terminal degree at the
master's level or lower.

Both among the librarians (16. 5%) and among the
faculty (18. 1%) some respondents qualified their replies arguing that no degree should be terminal or suggesting that educational requirements depend upon the position held. (This
is a valid point.   However, the survey instrument deliberately
refrained from making any suggestions as to what constitutes
basic requirements.   The intent was to discover what practitioners thought the basic preparation should be without attempting to influence them in any way.)

It is worth noting that 5. 4% of the librarians have the
doctorate, and 13. 4% anticipate earning that degree.   For the
terminal degree, 19. 6% of the librarians recommend the doctorate, which is nearly the same percentage as those who
have it or expect to earn it.   This may imply that librarians
tend to set requirements for terminal degrees mainly on the
basis of their own educational attainments and aspirations.
If this is the case, one might speculate that greater emphasis
may be placed on the doctorate for academic librarians as
more practitioners earn that degree.

As will be shown in the next chapter, those with degrees beyond the master's are likely to earn more and to
have a higher academic rank.   Consequently a number of aspects of the educational attainments and aspirations of librarians and faculty members were analyzed by applying the
chi-square test (see Table 41).   The differences are significant above the . 01 level in all cases.   Fewer librarians have
advanced degrees beyond the master's, fewer librarians expect to earn another degree, they feel less pressure to work
toward the doctorate, and they have lower expectations for
terminal degrees for librarians.

Publication and Research During the Past Two Years

Although it would be difficult to assess the quality of
the production, information on the number and types of pub-

TABLE 41

Educational Attainments and Aspirations of
Librarians and Faculty Members

	Librarians	Faculty
Hold master's degree or less	149	87
Hold graduate degree in addition to the master's	75	118

x^2 24. 7   df   1   P   . 001

Expect to earn another degree	71	63
Do not expect to earn another degree	121	22

Note: Those with the doctorate or who were undecided were
excluded.

x^2 13. 4   df   1   P   . 001

Under strong pressure to work toward the doctorate	17	101
Under no pressure to work toward the doctorate	143	44

x^2 112. 8   df   1   P   . 001

Recommend master's or less as terminal degree for librarians	74	43
Recommend another graduate degree beyond the master's as terminal degree for librarians	100	114

x^2 8. 1   df   1   P   . 01

lications of faculty members and librarians should be of some
value in determining their contributions to scholarship. Possibly some respondents exaggerated in reporting their publications, but one would expect all groups to act in essentially
the same fashion.

While the differences are considerable, a substantial
number in the current survey have published within the past
two years (see Tables 42 and 43). The average number of
publications of librarians was . 7, for the men it was 1. 2,
and for the women . 2. Of the total, 56 (37 men and 19
women) published during the past two years. For the faculty
the average number was 1. 7, exactly two for the men and
. 7 for the women. Of the total number of faculty members,
114 (103 men and 11 women) published.

TABLE 42

Publications During the Past Two Years
by Librarians by Sex

	Men		Women		Total	
	No. Items	% Who Pub- lished	No. Items	% Who Pub- lished	No. Items	% Who Pub- lished
Papers read at meetings	13	8. 0	7	6. 3	20	7. 1
Reviews of books, films, peri- odicals	53	12. 4	4	3. 6	57	8. 0
Journal articles	45	15. 9	3	2. 7	48	8. 9
Books edited	6	5. 3	2	1. 8	8	3. 1
Books written	3	1. 8	1	0. 9	4	1. 3
Miscellaneous[a]	12	3. 5	6	5. 4	18	4. 0
Total	132	32. 8[b]	23	17. 1[b]	155	25. 0[b]

[a]Includes editing journals, writing poetry and short
stories, film production, etc.

[b]Since some individuals published in more than one
area, percentages in the columns do not equal the totals.

TABLE 43

Publications During the Past Two Years
by Faculty Members by Sex

	Men		Women		Total	
	No. Items	% Who Pub- lished	No. Items	% Who Pub- lished	No. Items	% Who Pub- lished
Papers read at meetings	52	25. 9	4	9. 3	56	22. 4
Reviews of books, films, perio- odicals	85	14. 8	13	9. 3	98	13. 7
Journal articles	166	40. 7	8	11. 6	174	34. 6
Books edited	9	5. 6	1	2. 3	10	4. 9
Books written	10	5. 6	2	4. 7	12	5. 4
Miscellaneous[a]	7	3. 1	1	2. 3	8	2. 9
Total	329	63. 6[b]	29	25. 6	358	55. 6[b]

[a]Includes editing journals, writing poetry and short
stories, film productions, etc.

[b]Since some individuals published in more than one
area, percentages in the column do not equal the totals.

Few respondents have written books. In this area the
male faculty members are the most prolific; nine individuals
published a total of ten books. This group also leads in the
publishing of journal articles, in which area a comparatively
large number, 66 (40. 7%), reported contributions.

Those with the doctorate publish more. The faculty
men with that degree published an average of 2. 6 items compared with the . 9 items for those without it. Among the librarians the women with the doctorate published . 7 items,
which is equal to the total for the faculty women and more
than three times the quantity of the female librarians with
any other degree. The male librarians with the doctorate,

with an average of 5. 2 items, published more than any other
group, either faculty members or librarians.

   The 63. 6% of the male faculty members publishing in
some form is about at 2 1/2 times the 25. 6% of the female
faculty members, nearly twice the 32. 8% of the male librarians, and over 3 1/2 times the 17. 1% of the female librarians who published. Furthermore, the quantity of publication
of the male faculty members is considerably greater.   Next
are the male librarians, followed by the female faculty
members, and then by the female librarians.   To some extent the figures for the male librarians and faculty members
are enlarged by a few in each group who published a substantial amount.   Nevertheless, the men generally engage
more extensively in research and writing.   The average of
two items for the faculty men is more than double the . 7
items for the faculty women, and the average of 1. 2 items
for the men librarians is . 5 items above that for the faculty
women and six times the . 2 for the women librarians.

   Although none of the three female head librarians reported publications, the 14 male head librarians claimed an
average of 2. 9 items.   The average male head librarian is
more productive in this area than the average male faculty
members.

   The difference between the number of librarians and
faculty members who published is significant above the . 001
level (see Table 44).

TABLE 44

Number of Librarians and Faculty Members
Who Published During the Past Two Years

	Librarians	Faculty
Published	56	114
Did not publish	168	91

x^2 41. 6   df   1   P   . 001

Participation in Academic Government

To some extent at least, librarians look upon being voting members of the faculty, serving on academic committees, and being elected to the senate as an indication of acceptance by the faculty. In this respect the librarians in the current survey do comparatively well (see Table 45). ("Senate" and "faculty senate" are used here to designate any body which represents the entire institution and which has some voice in the government of that institution.)

TABLE 45

Faculty Members and Librarians as
Voting Members of the Faculty

	Faculty		Librarians	
	No.	%	No.	%
Voting member	196	95. 6	212	94. 6
Not a voting member	5	2. 4	11	4. 9
No response	4	2. 0	1	0. 5
Total	205	100. 0	224	100. 0

x^2 1. 7   df   1   P   . 20

The overwhelming majority, 212 (94. 6%), of the librarians are voting members of the faculty, as are 196 (95. 6%) of the faculty members. Why five of the latter do not have a vote is unclear.

Of the five librarians who do not have academic rank nor titles (see Chapter 7), only one (the head librarian) is a voting member of the faculty. Of those with equivalent rank, four reported being and two reported not being voting members. This, then, accounts for six of the 11 librarians who are not voting members of the faculty.

Apparently one or possibly two institutions do not have a faculty senate, but in those colleges and universities which do, nearly all of the librarians (85. 7%) and faculty members

(87. 6%) are eligible for election to that body (see Tables 46
and 47).   With 13. 4% of the librarians reporting that they are
members of the faculty senate as compared with 9. 8% of the
faculty, indications would seem to be that librarians are well
represented.   [Five (29. 4%) of the 17 head librarians reported
being members of the senate; but if these were taken out of
the totals, 25 or slightly more than 10% of the librarians
would still be members.]

TABLE 46

Eligibility for Election to the Faculty Senate and
Current Membership in That Body by Librarians by Sex

	Men		Women		Total	
	No.	%	No.	%	No.	%
Institution has no such body	7	6. 2	8	7. 2	15	6. 7
Eligible	99	87. 6	93	83. 8	192	85. 7
Not eligible	5	4. 4	7	6. 3	12	5. 4
Member of senate[a]	14	12. 4	16	14. 4	30	13. 4
No response	2	1. 8	3	2. 7	5	2. 2
Total	113	---	111	---	224	---

[a]Not included in totals because they are among those
who are eligible.

As far as service on academic committees is concerned librarians are less active.   Again, 213 (95. 1%) of the
librarians are eligible as are 96. 5% of the faculty (see
Tables 48 and 49).   Librarians reported serving on a total
of 130 committees and faculty members served on 178. While
36. 6% of the librarians served on one or more committees,
52. 2% of the faculty members did so.

To some degree, service on academic committees by
librarians is related to position.   Only three of the 17 head
librarians were not members of any committees.   The head
librarians also accounted for six of the ten librarians who

TABLE 47

Eligibility for Election to the Faculty Senate and Current
Membership in That Body by Faculty Members by Sex

	Men		Women		Total	
	No.	%	No.	%	No.	%
Institution has						
no such body	10	6. 1	4	9. 3	14	6. 8
Eligible	144	89. 0	36	83. 7	180	87. 8
Not eligible	7	4. 3	2	4. 7	9	4. 4
Member of senate[a]	17	10. 5	3	7. 0	20	9. 8
No response	1	0. 6	1	2. 3	2	1. 0
Total	162	---	43	---	205	

[a]Not included in totals because they are among those
who are eligible.

served on three or more committees, and for six of the 16
who were chairman of committees.

Among the other administrative positions such as associate director, department heads, or heads of divisional libraries, 42. 9% reported membership on committees as compared with 26. 4% of those who did not hold such positions.
However, not too much should be made of this because the
responses were not always precise. Some individuals simply
used such titles as circulation librarian or acquisitions librarian, which may, but need not mean, that they are the heads
of those services.

Lack of formal classification of librarians as academic
does not of itself mean automatic exclusion from participation
in faculty government. Two of the five faculty assistants and
assistant instructors said they were eligible for committee
assignment, as did four of the six with equivalent rank and
four of the five without rank or titles.

Librarians in the present survey fare less well with
regard to service on academic committees than they do with

TABLE 48

Eligibility for Election and Service on Academic
Committees by Librarians by Sex

	Men		Women		Total	
	No.	%	No.	%	No.	%
Eligible for election	110	97. 3	103	92. 8	213	95. 1
Not eligible	2	1. 8	4	3. 6	6	2. 7
Do not know	0		2	1. 8	2	0. 9
No response	1	0. 9	2	1. 8	3	1. 3
Not on any committee	69	61. 1	73	65. 8	142	63. 4
Total number on committees	44	38. 9	38	34. 2	82	36. 6
Member of one committee	29	25. 7	23	20. 7	52	23. 2
Member of two committees	9	8. 0	11	9. 9	20	8. 9
Member of three or more committees	6	5. 3	4	3. 6	10	4. 5
Chairman of a committee	10	8. 8	6	5. 4	16	7. 1

regard to the faculty senate. Presumably both senate and
committee memberships are indications of acceptance by the
faculty, although librarians may in some institutions elect
their own representative to the senate.

Participation in faculty government may be explained
to some extent on the basis of frequent association and close
acquaintance. Faculty members usually have regular contacts with others in their department or division just as librarians have more extensive relationships with other librarians. It would seem logical, then, that faculty members
would tend to nominate and elect those whom they know well
(that is, other faculty members), and this need not reflect a
rejection of the librarians but rather a preference for those

TABLE 49

Eligibility for Election and Service on Academic
Committees by Faculty Members by Sex

	Men		Women		Total	
	No.	%	No.	%	No.	%
Eligible for election	157	96. 9	41	95. 3	198	96. 5
Not eligible	3	1. 9	0	0. 0	3	1. 5
No response	2	1. 2	2	4. 7	4	2. 0
Not on any committee	69	42. 6	29	67. 4	98	47. 8
Total number on committees	93	57. 4	14	32. 6	107	52. 2
Member of one committee	55	34. 0	9	20. 9	64	31. 2
Member of two committees	23	14. 2	5	11. 6	28	13. 7
Member of three or more committees	15	9. 3	0		15	7. 3
Chairman of a committee	22	13. 6	2	4. 7	24	11. 7

whom they know more intimately.

Because of the large number of committees and because of the variations in names used at different institutions, it is not necessary to list them all here.   However,
it may be worth listing examples of committees which might
be of greatest concern to librarians (see Table 50).

On the committees on appointment, promotions, and
tenure; curriculum; publications; research; and student affairs, the faculty respondents reported more memberships
than the librarians.   In the other cases the librarians were
represented by an equal or greater number.   The faculty
members reported no memberships on the library building,
computer, media, or radio and television committees.   In

general it seems that librarians are represented rather well
on the important committees, at least in some institutions,
but there are no doubt many variations among the 19 institutions.

TABLE 50

Number of Faculty Members and Librarians
on a Selected Number of Committees

Committee Name[a]	No. Faculty Memberships	No. Librarian Memberships
Appointment, Promotions, and Tenure	8	5
Committee on Committees	5	5
Computer	0	1
Curriculum	16	9
Library	7	9
Library Building	0	3
Long Range Planning	3	3
Media	0	3
Publications	4	1
Radio and Television	0	2
Research	2	1
Sabbatical Leaves	1	1
Student Affairs	6	3

[a]At some institutions the committee may have a different name, but an effort was made to relate those committees which have a similar function regardless of the name
used by the respondent.

Professional Activity

Although some writers on higher education place little
emphasis on professional activity as criteria for promotion
and salary increments, many librarians tend to consider this
of marked importance. Consequently, a comparison of librarians and faculty members in this respect is of interest
(see Tables 51 and 52).

TABLE 51

Membership in Professional Associations
of Librarians by Sex

	Men		Women		Total	
	No.	%	No.	%	No.	%
National Associations						
None	45	39. 8	38	34. 2	83	37. 1
1	32	28. 4	37	33. 4	69	30. 8
2	18	15. 9	23	20. 7	41	18. 3
3 or more	18	15. 9	13	11. 7	31	13. 8
	113	100. 0	111	100. 0	224	100. 0
Regional Associations						
None	103	91. 1	103	92. 8	206	92. 0
1	8	7. 1	8	7. 2	16	7. 1
2	2	1. 8	0		2	0. 9
3 or more	0		0		0	
	113	100. 0	111	100. 0	224	100. 0
State Associations						
None	24	21. 2	42	37. 9	66	29. 5
1	45	39. 9	40	36. 0	85	38. 0
2	25	22. 1	20	18. 0	45	20. 1
3 or more	19	16. 8	9	8. 1	28	12. 4
	113	100. 0	111	100. 0	224	100. 0

Both on the national and regional levels faculty members hold more memberships in professional associations, but
librarians hold more on the state level.

Among the faculty, 85. 8% are members of one or more
national associations, compared with 62. 9% of the librarians.
Possibly some of the librarians have attended conferences of
the Midwest Academic Librarians, but that is not a formal
organization. Conferences are held but no one actually belongs to the association. Thus one would not expect many of

TABLE 52

Membership in Professional Associations of Faculty Members by Sex

	Men		Women		Total	
	No.	%	No.	%	No.	%
National Associations						
None	23	14. 2	6	14. 0	29	14. 2
1	31	19. 1	12	27. 8	43	21. 0
2	40	24. 7	14	32. 6	54	26. 3
3 or more	68	42. 0	11	25. 6	79	38. 5
	162	100. 0	43	100. 0	205	100. 0
Regional Associations						
None	118	72. 9	34	79. 1	152	74. 2
1	35	21. 6	9	20. 9	44	21. 5
2	8	4. 9	0		8	3. 8
3 or more	1	0. 6	0		1	0. 5
	162	100. 0	43	100. 0	205	100. 0
State Associations						
None	79	48. 8	17	39. 6	96	46. 8
1	61	37. 6	20	46. 5	81	39. 5
2	13	8. 0	5	11. 6	18	8. 8
3 or more	9	5. 6	1	2. 3	10	4. 9
	162	100. 0	43	100. 0	205	100. 0

the librarians to belong to a regional association since no such organization for librarians exists in the Midwest.

On the state level, librarians (70. 5%) are more likely to hold memberships in associations than are faculty members (53. 2%). Also, more librarians are members of three or more state associations than are faculty members, 12. 4% compared with 4. 9%.

As far as active participation in professional associa-

tions, in the form of committee memberships and serving as
officers, is concerned, the percentages are so small for all
groups as to make commentary unnecessary (see Tables 53
and 54).

TABLE 53

Membership on Committees and Offices Held in
Professional Associations by Librarians by Sex

	Men		Women		Total	
	No.	%	No.	%	No.	%
National Associations	4	3. 5	2	1. 8	6	2. 7
Regional Associations	1	0. 9	0		1	0. 5
State Associations	13	11. 5	5	4. 5	18	8. 0

TABLE 54

Membership on Committees and Offices Held in
Professional Associations by Faculty Members by Sex

	Men		Women		Total	
	No.	%	No.	%	No.	%
National Associations	8	4. 9	2	4. 7	10	4. 9
Regional Associations	6	3. 7	0		6	2. 9
State Associations	10	6. 2	2	4. 7	12	5. 9

Most professions have one major national association.
For librarians this is the American Library Association
(ALA).   For college and university teachers it is the American Association of University Professors (AAUP).   Teachers
also have what for the sake of convenience will be labeled
"subject associations" such as the American Historical Association, the American Economic Association, the American
Sociological Association, etc.   To give a more detailed view
of participation it may be of interest to show percentages of
membership in a few of these organizations (see Tables 55
and 56).

While 43. 8% of the librarians are members of ALA,
83. 4% of the faculty belong to a national subject association.
Again, with but a few exceptions, membership by sex shows
more similarities than differences.   Curiously, however,
11. 5% more of the women than men librarians belong to ALA
whereas 8. 5% more of the faculty men belong to a national
subject association than do the faculty women.   Nearly one
of every four (24. 6%) of the librarians belongs to a subject
association, which represents a membership more than half
as large as that for ALA, but few of them joined the Special
Libraries Association (SLA), the National Education Association's Department of Audio-Visual Instruction (DAVI), or the
American Society for Information Science (ASIS).

Just under 19% of the librarians belong to AAUP, as
compared with 30. 7% of the faculty.   In this case a larger
percentage of the faculty women (53. 5%) belong than do
faculty men (24. 7%).

Sex

Since differences by sex are discussed throughout the
survey, this section serves as a general summary rather
than a detailed analysis.

Educational differences between men and women are
conspicuous.   The men have both more and higher degrees.
Fewer women feel pressure to work toward the doctorate.
The male librarians who do not have the doctorate have
earned an average of 22. 3 semester credits beyond their
highest degree, and the female librarians 10. 1 credits.

Among the faculty far more men (65. 4%) than women
(27. 9%) have the doctorate.   The faculty men without that

TABLE 55

Membership of Librarians in Certain National Associations

	Men		Women		Total	
	No.	%	No.	%	No.	%
ALA	43	38. 1	55	49. 6	98	43. 8
AAUP	21	18. 6	21	18. 9	42	18. 8
SLA	3	2. 7	3	2. 7	6	2. 7
ASIS	1	0. 9	1	0. 9	2	0. 9
DAVI	6	5. 3	0	0. 0	6	2. 7
Subject Associations[a]	30	25. 6	25	22. 5	55	24. 6

[a]"Subject association" is used here to designate organizations such as the American Historical Association, the Modern Language Association, the National Education Association, etc.

TABLE 56

Membership of Faculty Members in Certain National Associations

	Men		Women		Total	
	No.	%	No.	%	No.	%
AAUP	40	24. 7	23	53. 5	63	30. 7
Subject Associations	138	85. 2	33	76. 7	171	83. 4

degree have earned an average of 36. 2 semester credits beyond their highest degree and the faculty women 21.

During the past two years the men in the sample

published more than the women.   This is true both among
the faculty and librarians.   On the average the male head
librarians and the male librarians with the doctorate were
more productive in publishing than any other group.   The
female head librarians reported no publications, and the women librarians as a group were well below the average of
the female faculty members, the male librarians, and the
male faculty members.   While less productive than the male
faculty member, the average male librarian published more
than the average female faculty member.

A smaller proportion of the female librarians is in
the 31 to 50 age span than is the case for either the male
librarians or the male faculty members.

Differences between men and women are evident with
regard to rank, salaries, and sabbaticals.   These factors
will receive further attention in the next chapter.

Faculty men have been more likely to receive sabbatical leaves than any other group.   Next are male librarians
followed by female librarians and then female faculty members.   The pattern for faculty rank and for salaries is similar.   The faculty men are more likely to be in the higher
academic ranks, and their average salary is higher than any
other group.   With regard to rank and salaries the male librarians are second, then the female faculty members, and
the female librarians are the lowest group.

In summary, then, women tend to receive lower compensation in the form of salaries, sabbaticals, and rank.
However, in drawing conclusions from this, one must also
consider background and contributions.   Only a small percentage of the female faculty members, for example, have
been in higher education or at their present institution long
enough to become eligible for a sabbatical under the usual
policies whereby the recipient must have tenure and, in many
cases, at least six years service at that institution.   Similarly, the great majority of the faculty women have not been
at their institution long enough to be eligible for promotion
to one of the two highest academic ranks.   For the female
librarians the lower educational level and meager publication
record are probably serious handicaps to advancement.

Chapter 7

Benefit of Faculty Status

Faculty rank has been of interest to librarians for many years; but recently librarians became increasingly concerned about the benefits of faculty status, including commensurate salaries, sabbaticals and other leaves, tenure, travel funds, vacations, and time and funds for research and writing. This chapter reports the results of the survey with regard to these factors.

Faculty Rank

In the current survey 208 (92. 9%) of the librarians have academic rank, five (2. 2%) do not have it, six (2. 7%) have equivalent rank, and five (2. 2%) are faculty assistants or assistant instructors (see Tables 57 and 58). Although they may be part of the faculty, in most institutions the latter group are not considered permanent employees unless or until they earn additional degrees or meet other criteria for appointment to one of the traditional academic ranks. These five individuals were included in the survey because their names were submitted by the head librarians. Persons with the same title and possibly with similar background are employed on the teaching staff in the various institutions, but these were excluded from the faculty survey.

While nearly all of the librarians in the survey have academic rank, few of them are in the upper levels. More than five times the percentage of faculty members hold the rank of professor, 19. 5% of the faculty and 3. 6% of the librarians. More than 2 1/2 times the percentage of librarians are at the level of instructor, 49. 1% of the librarians and 19% of the faculty. In the intermediate ranks, 9. 9% more faculty members are assistant professors and 11. 4% more are associate professors.

Part of the difference in the percentage of faculty members and librarians in the various ranks can probably

TABLE 57

Academic Rank of Librarians by Sex

	Men		Women		Total	
	No.	%	No.	%	No.	%
No rank nor title	2	1. 8	3	2. 7	5	2. 2
Equivalent rank	3	2. 7	3	2. 7	6	2. 7
Assistant inst. or faculty assistant	0		5	4. 5	5	2. 2
Instructor	50	44. 2	60	54. 1	110	49. 1
Assistant professor	32	28. 3	29	26. 1	61	27. 2
Associate professor	18	15. 9	11	9. 9	29	13. 0
Professor	8	7. 1	0		8	3. 6
Total	113	100. 0	111	100. 0	224	100. 0

TABLE 58

Academic Rank of Faculty Members by Sex

	Men		Women		Total	
	No.	%	No.	%	No.	%
Instructor	22	13. 6	17	39. 5	39	19. 0
Assistant professor	55	33. 9	21	48. 9	76	37. 1
Associate professor	46	28. 4	4	9. 3	50	24. 4
Professor	39	24. 1	1	2. 3	40	19. 5
Total	162	100. 0	43	100. 0	205	100. 0

be explained on the basis of education.   Among faculty members the percentage with the doctorate increases with each higher rank (see Table 59).   It is worth noting that all the

TABLE 59

Academic Rank of Faculty Members with the Doctorate

	Total Number	Number with Doctorate	Percentage with Doctorate
Instructor	39	1	2. 6
Assistant professor	76	35	46. 0
Associate professor	50	42	84. 0
Professor	40	40	100. 0
Total	205	118	

TABLE 60

Academic Rank of Librarians with the Doctorate

	Total Number	Number with Doctorate	Percentate with Doctorate
Instructor	110	0	0. 0
Assistant professor	61	2	3. 3
Associate professor	29	5	17. 2
Professor	8	5	62. 5
Total	208	12	

faculty members with the rank of professor have the doctorate, as do 84% of the associate professors, 46% of the assistant professors, and 2.6% of the instructors.

For librarians either the doctorate or a high administrative position is related to the rank of professor (see Table 60). Five (62. 5%) of the librarians with that rank have the doctorate, and of these five, three are library directors and two are assistant directors in charge of technical services. The three other librarians with the rank of professor are also directors of libraries and have two master's degrees.

Thus, while the doctorate shows a perfect relationship with the rank of professor for faculty members in the present survey, this is not the case for librarians.

Furthermore, in contrast to the 42 of 50 (84%) of the faculty members who are associate professors and who have the doctorate, five of the 29 (17. 2%) of the librarians with that rank have that degree. At the assistant professor level, 35 of 76 (46%) of the faculty members have the doctorate, and the same applies to two (3. 3%) of the 61 librarians.

Whether discrimination against women exists is not clear. Considerable differences exist in rank between men and women, both among faculty members and librarians. None of the female librarians is a professor, and only one faculty woman holds that rank. Similarly a smaller percentage of the faculty women are at the associate professor level, but proportionately more are at the assistant professor and instructor levels. Among the librarians the percentage of women is greater than that for men only at the level of instructor. To some extent this may result from differences in educational level and publication, for as a group the male faculty members and librarians both have more education and publish more than do their female colleagues. Of the 106 faculty men with the doctorate, 39, or more than one of every three, is a professor; of the 12 faculty women with the doctorate, only one is a professor. In fact, the male librarians have more chance of being promoted to the higher ranks without the doctorate than do faculty women with it. While 8% of the male librarians have the doctorate, 7. 1% are professors and 15. 9% are associate professors. Although 27. 9% of the female faculty members have the doctorate, 2. 3% are professors and 9. 3% are associate professors. However, the faculty women also have less experience (60. 5% with five years or under) and have been at their institutions for a short time (83. 7% with five years or under). These factors may explain most of the difference.

Since all but 16 of the librarians reported having faculty rank and titles, no major conclusions can be drawn from the results. Nevertheless, it may be of interest to mention a few of the differences between those who do and those who do not have faculty rank and titles.

With regard to certain critical factors, not having faculty rank seems to make a difference. This is particularly true in relation to tenure, salaries, and sabbaticals.

None of the five without faculty rank and titles, which included one head librarian and four staff positions in both
public and technical services, reported being eligible for
tenure or for sabbaticals.   Their average compensation is
lower, but more will be said about this in the section on
salaries.   Only the head librarian was a voting member of
the faculty, but four of the five reported being eligible for
service on academic committees.   One was on the academic
calendar committee and one was on the library committee.
Although other institutional factors might account for the situation, it may be of interest to note that three of the staff
members have been at their present institution for less than
a year, and the fourth has been there for less than two years.
The head librarian has been there for more than five years.
One of the five reported a publication which consisted of a
paper read at a professional meeting.

Examining those six with equivalent rank shows less
consistency.   Four of the six reported being voting members
of the faculty and being eligible for tenure, and five said
they were eligible for sabbatical leaves.   With regard to
other factors these six are generally similar to those who
have faculty rank.

Of the five with titles of assistant instructor or faculty
assistant, one had the fifth-year bachelor's degree in library
science, which evidently was not accepted in that institution as
the equivalent of the fifth-year master's degree.   The other
four held the bachelor's as the highest degree, and three of
them had taken additional course work, one with 18 credits
and two with four each.   One of the five reported being eligible for tenure, two said they were eligible for service on
academic committees, and one of these was on the faculty
social committee.   Three were voting members of the faculty, and one of the five said she was eligible for sabbatical
leaves.

Sabbaticals and Other Leaves

Sabbatical Leaves

In many colleges and smaller universities sabbaticals
are used to assist those who are working toward advanced
degrees, but frequently only a small number of leaves are
available each year.   That funds are limited would seem to
be the case in these 19 institutions (see Tables 61 and 62).

TABLE 61

Sabbatical Leaves Received by Librarians by Sex

	Men		Women		Total	
	No.	%	No.	%	No.	%
Have received sabbaticals	8	7.1	6	5.4	14[a]	6.3
Have not received sabbaticals	105	92.9	105	94.6	210	93.7
Total	113	100.0	111	100.0	224	100.0

[a]Of these, three (1.4%) reported summer leaves, apparently with pay.

TABLE 62

Sabbatical Leaves Received by Faculty Members by Sex

	Men		Women		Total	
	No.	%	No.	%	No.	%
Have received sabbaticals	17	10.5	2	4.7	19	9.3
Have not received sabbaticals	145	89.5	41	95.3	186	90.7
Total	162	100.0	43	100.0	205	100.0

Only a very small number of librarians, 11 (4.9%) have had sabbatical leaves; and three more (1.4%) reported such leaves for the summer, apparently with salary, for a total of 6.3%. (As indicated by respondents, two librarians in Wisconsin are currently on leave with pay to work toward advanced degrees, but they are not included in the survey.)

TABLE 63

Eligibility of Librarians for Sabbatical Leaves by Sex

	Men		Women		Total	
	No.	%	No.	%	No.	%
Yes	73	64. 6	64	57. 7	137	61. 2
No	35	31. 0	36	32. 4	71	31. 6
Do not know	1	0. 9	7	6. 3	8	3. 6
No response	4	3. 5	4	3. 6	8	3. 6
Total	113	100. 0	111	100. 0	224	100. 0

TABLE 64

Eligibility of Faculty Members for Sabbatical
Leaves by Sex

	Men		Women		Total	
	No.	%	No.	%	No.	%
Yes	103	63. 6	26	60. 5	129	62. 9
No	48	29. 6	15	34. 9	63	30. 7
Do not know	5	3. 1	1	2. 3	6	3. 0
No response	6	3. 7	1	2. 3	7	3. 4
Total	162	100. 0	43	100. 0	205	100. 0

Although more faculty members have had sabbaticals, the total is still small, 19 (9. 3%). More than twice as large a percentage of the faculty men (10. 5%) have had sabbatical leaves as did the women (4. 7%). In fact, a larger percentage of both the male (7. 1%) and female librarians (5. 4%) have had such leaves than have the faculty women (4. 7%).

As far as eligibility for sabbaticals is concerned, the

percentages for the faculty and librarians are almost identical
(see Tables 63 and 64). Unfortunately the results are com-
plicated somewhat by the fact that the Wisconsin State University system has "teacher improvement leaves" rather than
sabbaticals. Consequently the percentages for eligibility
would probably be considerably higher if "teacher improvement leaves" had been included as a possible response. However, because results are so similar, 62.9% for the faculty
and 61.2% for librarians, there is very little if any discrimination against librarians in this area except for the five librarians who do not have faculty rank. Of these none was
eligible.

Possibly the most conspicuous result is that so few of
the respondents have had leaves with pay that this is a
meager benefit to any group. Additional funds are needed
for both librarians and faculty members to make this opportunity more widely available.

However, another factor is also involved and may
partially explain the results. Naturally the age, years of
experience, and time at the institution are related to whether
a person has received a sabbatical. A large proportion of
the respondents have been in college and university librarianship or teaching for five years or fewer. This ranges
from 36.5% of the faculty men to 60.5% of the faculty women, 45.2% of the male, and 45.9% of the female librarians.
An even larger percentage have been at their institution for
five years or fewer, 65.8% of the women librarians, 79.7%
of the men librarians, 66.1% of the faculty men, and 83.7%
of the women faculty.

Thus, because of the lack of experience and short
term of service, many of them could not have received
leaves under the traditional systems which normally require
six years of service before receiving a sabbatical.

Leaves of Absence Without Salary

Since no direct monetary incentive is connected with
leaves of absences without salary, the person who takes such
a leave to continue his education probably has a rather high
motivation to work toward an advanced degree.

It is worthy of note that more than twice as many respondents have taken leaves of absences without salary as
have received sabbaticals (see Tables 65 and 66). Among the

TABLE 65

Leaves of Absence Without Salary Taken by
Librarians by Sex

	Men		Women		Total	
	No.	%	No.	%	No.	%
None	95	84. 0	96	86. 5	191	85. 2
One	14	12. 4	10	9. 0	24	10. 7
Two or more	3	2. 7	5	4. 5	8	3. 6
No response	1	0. 9	0	0. 0	1	0. 5
Total	113	100. 0	111	100. 0	224	100. 0

TABLE 66

Leaves of Absence Without Salary Taken
by Faculty Members by Sex

	Men		Women		Total	
	No.	%	No.	%	No.	%
None	129	79. 6	35	81. 4	164	80. 0
One	28	17. 3	6	14. 0	34	16. 6
Two or more	5	3. 1	2	4. 6	7	3. 4
Total	162	100. 0	43	100. 0	205	100. 0

faculty members 9. 3% have received sabbaticals but 20% have taken leaves without pay. While the figures for the faculty men are 10. 5% and 20. 4%, or nearly double for leaves without pay, among the faculty women nearly four times as many have taken leaves without pay, 18. 6% without pay compared with 4. 7% with it.

For the librarians the situation is similar; 6. 3% have had sabbaticals and 14. 3% have taken leaves without salary.

For the men the figures are 7. 1% and 15. 1% respectively for
leaves with and without pay.   For the women the percentages
are 5. 4 and 13. 5.

The differences between librarians and faculty members regarding eligibility for sabbaticals, for sabbaticals received, and for leaves of absences taken are not statistically
significant at the . 05 level (see Table 67).

TABLE 67

Sabbaticals Received, Eligibility for Sabbaticals, and
Leaves of Absence Taken by Librarians and
Faculty Members

	Librarians	Faculty
Had sabbatical leave	14	19
Did not have sabbatical leave	210	186

x^2 1. 4   df   1   P   . 30

| Eligible for sabbaticals | 137 | 129 |
| Not eligible for sabbaticals | 71 | 63 |

x^2 0. 1   df   1   P   . 80

| Have taken leaves of absence | 32 | 41 |
| Have not taken leaves of absence | 191 | 164 |

x^2 2. 4   df   1   P   . 20

Commensurate Salaries

Salaries are a major concern and are examined from
several perspectives including education, rank, and scholarly

activity.   Because the education of the librarians with the
sixth-year degree and those with two master's degrees is
broadly comparable to that of faculty members with the master's degree, these groups were singled out for statistical
analysis.   The Mann-Whitney U-test, which is designed to
determine whether the medians of two groups are similar,
was used.   A z value greater than ± 1.96 is significant at
the .05 level and indicates that the chance of the medians
being the same is small.

Since virtually all of the faculty members and over
half of the librarians are on nine-month contracts, averages
were calculated on a nine-month basis.   Generally librarians
tend to argue that they are underpaid in comparison with the
faculty.   Looking at the overall averages definitely gives the
impression that this is the case (see Table 68).

TABLE 68

Average Salaries of Faculty Members and
Librarians by Sex

	Men		Women		Total	
	No.	Salaries	No.	Salaries	No.	Salaries
Faculty members	162	$12,170	43	$9,843	205	$11,682
Librarians	113	9,993	111	8,795	224	9,399
Difference		2,177		1,048		2,283

The average salary of the librarians is $2,283 less
than that of the faculty.   However, the difference is more
pronounced for the men than it is for the women, with the
male librarian's salary being $2,177 lower than that of the
male faculty member, but the female librarian's, $1,048 be-
low the average for the female faculty members.   This does
not mean that female librarians are more adequately paid.
It simply indicates that the salaries of both female librarians
and faculty members are lower.   In fact, even though their
salaries are $2,177 below those of male faculty members,
the average for the male librarians is $150 above that of the

female faculty members.

Given the fact that institutional practices vary and
that many considerations may enter into the determination of
salaries, it is still possible to make more precise comparisons than just overall averages.   Consequently the present
questionnaire was designed to garner information on a number of details.   Are salaries related to degrees?   Does publishing make a difference?   To what extent is salary related
to rank?   Answers to these questions give a clearer understanding of how well librarians fare in comparison with
faculty members.

That the institutions in the survey reward those with
the doctorate is shown by the salary differences between
those with and without that degree (see Tables 69 and 70).
The average salary for the faculty members with the doctorate is $13, 229 compared with $9, 605 for those with the
master's degree, even though many in the latter group are
well on their way toward the doctorate.   For the total faculty
sample this represents $3, 624 more for the doctorate.
Among the men, those with the doctorate earn $4, 437 more
than those with the master's, and among the women the difference is $2, 834.

Among the librarians the situation is similar.   Those
with the doctorate earn an average of $2, 032 more than
those with the sixth-year degree, $3, 187 more than those
with two master's degrees, and $4, 328 more than those with
only the master's degree.

The male librarians with the doctorate earn somewhat
less than male faculty members with that degree, a difference
of $404.   The male librarians with a doctorate have a salary
advantage of $3, 042 over those with the sixth-year degree,
$3, 561 over those with two master's degrees, and $4, 667
over those with only the master's degree.

For the women the degree alone is less of an advantage.   Except for those female librarians with the sixth-year
degree, the salaries of women in all categories is consistently lower than it is for the men.   The faculty women earn
an average of $2, 327 less than faculty men.   Faculty women
with the doctorate earn $2, 404 less than the faculty men
with that degree; and among librarians the inequity is even
greater because women librarians with the doctorate earn an
average of $3, 000 less than male librarians with the docto-

TABLE 69

Average Salaries of Librarians by Degrees and Sex

	Men		Women		Total	
	No.	Salary	No.	Salary	No.	Salary
Doctorate	9	$13,917	3	$10,917	12	$13,167
Sixth-year degree	4	10,875	9	11,250	13	11,135
Two master's	33	10,356	17	9,250	50	9,980
Master's	65	9,250	76	8,487	141	8,839
Bachelor's	2	8,750	6	6,667	8	7,188
Total average:	--	9,993	--	8,795	--	9,399

TABLE 70

Average Salaries of Faculty Members
by Degrees and Sex

	Men		Women		Total	
	No.	Salary	No.	Salary	No.	Salary
Doctorate	106	$14,321	12	$11,917	118	$13,229
Master's	56	9,884	30	9,083	86	9,605
Bachelor's	0	-----	1	7,750	1	7,750
Total average:	--	12,170	--	9,842	--	11,682

rate. Furthermore, women librarians with the doctorate
still earn an average $333 less than those female librarians
with the sixth-year degree and only $42 more than the men
with that degree. However, they earn $1,667 more than
women with two master's degrees and $2,430 more than
those with only the master's. In making comparisons with
the faculty members, having the doctorate is still an advantage for female librarians because they earn an average
of $1,033 more than faculty men with the master's degree

and $1, 834 more than faculty women with the master's degree.

In summary, then, those with the doctorate earn substantially more on the average than those who do not have it. For the faculty, having the doctorate represents a salary advantage of $3, 624 over those with the master's degree, but for the men it is $4, 437 above the other men whereas for the women it is only $2, 834 over the women and $2, 033 over the men with only the master's. The male librarians with the doctorate earn an average of $4, 667 more than male librarians with only the master's, but for the female librarians the salary advantage is but slightly more than half that amount or $2, 430 over female librarians with only the master's degree.

Computing the salary advantage for an arbitrary period of ten years for the various degrees held by librarians will lend perspective to the salary differences. Using results from the survey and without considering possible fluctuations or other factors which influence salaries, one can arrive at figures which may be suggestive.

If the doctorate requires three full years of study, the candidate would forego $26, 517 in salary, or three times the average of $8, 839 earned by librarians with the master's degree. But for the ten years after he earns his degree he would earn an average of $4, 328 more per year or $43, 280. With the doctorate, then, he would have the potential to earn $16, 763 for the ten-year period above and beyond the three-year loss of salary.

Assuming that the second master's degree requires a year of study, one would then expect the librarian to forego $8, 839 in salary. During the next ten years he could expect to earn $11, 410 more, or ten times the $1, 141 difference between the average salary for those with the master's and with two master's degrees. Over the next ten years he would potentially earn $2, 571 above the loss of a year's salary. The sixth-year degree also normally requires one full year of study, but the salary advantage over having the master's is $2, 296 for one year or $22, 960 for ten years. The gain over the ten years would then be $14, 121 beyond the loss of a year's salary.

Examining remuneration in this fashion shows but a slight monetary advantage for the second master's, but the sixth-year degree and the doctorate represent definite salary advantages.

That the average salary of librarians is lower than that of faculty members is true. Nevertheless, when degrees are considered, the salary of librarians and faculty members is similar, and in a few instances librarians have a slight advantage (see Table 71). The salary advantages of the librarians with two master's degrees or with the sixth-year degree is statistically significant above the .01 level.

As shown in Table 33, the average faculty member with the master's degree has earned 30.9 additional semester credits, which may be considered roughly equivalent to the requirements for a master's degree. Thus the librarians who have two master's degrees or the sixth-year certificate have approximately the same amount of formal education as does the average faculty member without the doctorate, and the two groups may be considered roughly comparable. The eight faculty members and three librarians who have completed all requirements for the doctorate except the dissertation have somewhat more education than the equivalent of the master's degree, but they are included in the calculations.

The librarians with two master's degrees earn on the average $375 more than the faculty members with the master's as the highest degree. For the male librarians the difference is $472 and for the female it is $167. Having the sixth-year degree is a considerable advantage to the women librarians, for the average salary of that group is $2,167 above that of the female faculty members with the master's degree and $1,366 above the male faculty members with the master's degree. Generally, then, the librarians with two master's degrees or the sixth-year degree earn more than the faculty members with the master's as the highest degree.

Taking only those librarians with the master's as the highest degree shows the opposite results, for the faculty members are above the librarians in all cases, the male faculty members above the male librarians by $634 and the female faculty members above the female librarians by $596.

The relationship between rank and salary is more pronounced than that between salary and degrees (see Tables 72 and 73). This is probably the case because the doctorate itself seems to be an important factor in advancement in

TABLE 71

Average Salaries of Faculty Members with the Master's
as the Highest Degree Compared with Librarians with
Two Master's Degrees, with the Sixth-Year Degree,
and the Master's Degree

	Men		Women		Total[a]	
	No.	Salary	No.	Salary	No.	Salary
Librarians with two master's	32	$10,356	18	$9,250	50	$9,980
Faculty members with master's	56	9,884	30	9,083	86	9,605
Salary difference		472		167		375
Z 2.7 P .01						
Librarians with sixth-year degree	4	$10,875	9	$11,250	13	$11,135
Faculty members with master's	56	9,884	30	9,083	86	9,605
Salary difference		991		2,167		1,530
Z 3.0 P .01						
Faculty members with master's	56	$ 9,884	30	$ 9,083	86	$9,605
Librarians with only one master's	66	9,250	75	8,487	141	8,839
Salary difference		634		596		766
Z 2.6 P .01						

[a]The statistical significance was calculated only for the
total groups, not for the men and women separately.

rank for faculty members. All the faculty members who are
professors also have the doctorate, as do 84% of the associate professors, 46% of the assistant professors, and 2. 6%
of the instructors.

TABLE 72

Average Salaries of Librarians by Rank and Sex

	Men		Women		Total	
	No.	Salary	No.	Salary	No.	Salary
Professor	8	$14, 938	0	$	8	$14, 938
Associate prof.	18	12, 639	11	12, 568	29	12, 612
Assistant prof.	32	9, 875	29	9, 491	61	9, 693
Instructor	50	8, 480	60	7, 983	110	8, 209
Asst. inst. &						
faculty asst.	0		5	6, 850	5	6, 850
Equivalent rank	3	8, 917	3	8, 083	6	8, 500
Without rank	2	7, 750	3	8, 417	5	8, 150
Total average		9, 993		8, 795		9, 399

TABLE 73

Average Salaries of Faculty Members by Rank and Sex

	Men		Women		Total	
	No.	Salary	No.	Salary	No.	Salary
Professor	39	$15, 635	1	$14, 750	40	$15, 613
Associate prof.	46	12, 978	4	13, 625	50	13, 030
Assistant prof.	55	10, 477	21	10, 060	76	10, 362
Instructor	22	8, 568	17	8, 338	39	8, 494
Total average		12, 170		9, 843		11, 682

More librarians are at the instructor level and conversely fewer are at the assistant, associate, and professor
levels. Although some librarians have been promoted to the

higher ranks without the doctorate, their sparse representation in the higher ranks may result from the small number
who have that degree.

   In each case the salary of librarians is lower than for
faculty members when comparisons are made rank by rank.
Inequities range from a low of $88 between male faculty
members and male librarians at the instructor level to a high
of $1,057 between the faculty women and female librarians
at the associate professor level. As for salary ranges, the
differences between the average for instructors and professors is $7,067 for the faculty men, $6,412 for the faculty
women, and $6,458 for the male librarians. Among female
librarians, none has the rank of professor but the average
associate professor earns $4,585 more than the instructor.

   Because but five librarians do not have faculty rank
and six have equivalent rank it is necessary to note that the
differences between them and the total sample may reflect
institutional variations rather than actual divergence from the
others in the sample. (The assumption that all those with
equivalent rank are from one institution and all those without
faculty rank are from another institution is based on letters
from the head librarians at those institutions and on comments made by respondents on the questionnaire.) Consequently, the following remarks are in the nature of speculation rather than assertion. The five librarians without faculty rank and titles receive an average of $59 less than the
instructors, but those with equivalent rank receive $291 more.
This would seem to indicate that faculty rank and titles make
little difference as far as salaries are concerned. However,
if these individuals had academic rank and titles, some of
them might be in a higher rank and the salary differences
might be greater than is indicated by a comparison with only
the instructors. When matched against the average salaries
for all librarians, those with equivalent rank are lower by
$899, and those without rank are lower by $1,249.

   Both among the faculty and the librarians those who
publish earn more (see Tables 74 and 75). For the librarians the difference is $1,384, and for faculty members it is
$1,379. Publishing represents the greatest advantage for the
male librarians who earn $1,627 more than the non-publish-
ing male librarians. The female librarian who published
earns $454 more than women librarians who did not. The
male faculty members who published during the past two
years receive an average of $901 more per year than their

TABLE 74

Average Salaries of Librarians Who Published
During the Past Two Years by Sex

	Men		Women		Total	
	No.	Salary	No.	Salary	No.	Salary
Published	37	$11,088	19	$9,171	56	$10,438
Did not publish	76	9,461	92	8,717	168	9,054
Difference		1,627		454		1,384

TABLE 75

Average Salaries of Faculty Members Who Published
During the Past Two Years by Sex

	Men		Women		Total	
	No.	Salary	No.	Salary	No.	Salary
Published	103	$12,498	11	$10,386	114	$12,294
Did not publish	59	11,597	32	9,656	91	10,915
Difference		901		730		1,379

male colleagues, and the female faculty members who published receive $730 more than theirs.   Thus writing shows most benefit for male librarians and male faculty members but much less for female faculty members and female librarians.   It is important to note that none of the female librarians and few of the female faculty members published more than one or, at best, two items.

Tenure

As librarians become more involved in research and publication, academic government, and the government of the library itself, tenure will become an increasingly important issue. In this regard librarians receive favorable treatment (see Table 76).

TABLE 76

Eligibility for Tenure by Faculty Members and Librarians

	Faculty Members		Librarians	
	No.	%	No.	%
Eligible for tenure	184	89. 8	200	89. 3
Not eligible	14	6. 8	19	8. 5
Do not know	1	0. 5	2	0. 9
No response	6	2. 9	3	1. 3
Total	205	100. 0	224	100. 0

x^2 0. 2   df   1   P   . 90

The percentage of faculty members and librarians who answered that they are eligible for tenure was almost identical, 89. 8% and 89. 3% respectively. Of the five librarians without faculty rank none reported being eligible for tenure. Among those with equivalent rank, two said no and four said yes, while four of those with the rank of assistant instructor or faculty assistant gave a negative response.

Among the 14 faculty members who said they were ineligible for tenure were 11 instructors and three assistant professors. One of them had the doctorate, so he must have been ineligible for reasons other than the degree. For some of the other 13 the reason for not being eligible for tenure was the lack of the doctorate. The requirements vary, for the responses indicate that in some institutions faculty members are eligible for tenure without the doctorate whereas this is required in others. For librarians the doctorate generally does not seem to be required for tenure which indicates that exceptions are apparently made for librarians.

If the doctorate were required for librarians to become eligible for tenure, only a small percentage would
qualify. It would seem, then, that at present librarians
have an advantage with regard to criteria for tenure.

Term of Contract and Vacations of Librarians

Some librarians place great emphasis on academic vacations as an inducement to study and research. This topic
also deserves some attention. Because 96. 6% or virtually
all of them are on nine-month contracts, the faculty will be
excluded from this discussion. Two of every three librarians are on a nine- or ten-month contract (see Tables 77 and
78). Among the women 69. 4% are employed on that basis,
and this applies to only 55. 8% of the men. Because of the
differences between men and women in publication and level
of education, the percentage of those on nine- or ten-month
and 12-month appointments needs to be kept in mind.

If rigid work schedules and shorter vacations are a
hindrance to professional development, one might then expect
to find greater scholarly activity and a higher level of education among those who have academic year contracts and
vacations.

TABLE 77

Term of Contract of Librarians by Sex

	Men		Women		Total	
	No.	%	No.	%	No.	%
9-10 month	72	55. 8	77	69. 4	149	66. 5
12 month	41	44. 2	34	30. 6	75	33. 5
Total	113	100. 0	111	100. 0	224	100. 0

In the current survey a slightly higher proportion of
the total sample on 12-month contracts published, 28% com-

TABLE 78

Vacations of Librarians

	No.	%
All	137	61. 2
None	67	29. 9
Partial[a]	17	7. 6
No response	3	1. 3
Total	224	100. 0

[a]Some of those on 12 month contracts get some academic vacations, and some of those who are on nine or ten month contracts must work part of the vacations (Christmas and spring vacation, for example) evidently in order to insure some level of continuing service during the holidays. Since the nine or ten month contracts provide the possibility of two to three months in the summer, all comparisons will be made on the basis of nine to ten and 12 month contracts.

---

pared with 23. 5% for those on nine- to ten-month appointments (see Table 79). For the total sample the results are not statistically significant at the . 05 level. Of the men, 37. 1% on 12-month contracts published, compared with 30. 6% of those on nine or ten months. Among the women a smaller margin of 17. 6 to 16. 8% respectively published.

Those with academic year appointments are no more productive than those who are employed for the full year (see Table 80). If carried to several decimal points the figures for those on nine- or ten-month contracts show a very slight advantage, but the differences are minor. Thus writing and research of the librarians in these institutions depend more on the individual than on term of contract.

Another consideration is whether there is any relationship between the term of contract and the educational aspirations of librarians. In the total sample a slightly larger proportion of those on 12-month contracts expect to earn another degree (see Table 81), but the results were not statistically significant. A larger percentage of the men on

TABLE 79

Librarians Who Published During the Past Two Years
by Term of Contract and Sex[a]

	Men		Women		Total[b]	
	No.	%	No.	%	No.	%
9-10 month	22	30. 6	13	16. 8	35	23. 5
12 month	15	37. 1	6	17. 6	21	28. 0

[a]Percentages refer to the proportion of those on nine or ten and 12 month contracts who published.

[b]Computations were done only for the total sample.

X^2 . 5   df   1   P   . 50

TABLE 80

Average Number of Items Published by Librarians
During the Past Two Years by Term of Contract by Sex

	Men	Women	Total
9-10 month	1. 2	0. 2	0. 7
12 month	1. 1	0. 2	0. 7

TABLE 81

Librarians Who Expect to Earn Another Degree
by Term of Contract and Sex

	Men		Women		Total[a]	
	No.	%	No.	%	No.	%
9-10 month	24	33. 3	20	25. 9	44	29. 5
12 month	13	31. 7	14	41. 2	27	36. 0

Note: Percentages refer to the proportion of those on
nine- or ten- and 12-month contracts.   Those with the
doctorate were excluded from the table.

[a]Computations were done only for the total sample.

X^2 1. 5   df   1   P   . 30

nine-month and of the women on 12-month contracts expect to
earn another degree.

In summary, then, having academic year contracts
does not result in a larger amount of writing nor does it
show a relationship with expectations for advanced degrees.
The individual librarian sets his standards without regard to
these factors.

Time and Funds for Publication and Research

At least to some extent one might expect research and
writing to be connected with the amount of time and money
provided to support such activities.

The percentage of affirmative replies from faculty
members (93. 2%) would seem to indicate that nearly all if
not all of the colleges and universities provide funds, and
the negative responses from librarians (20. 1%) would seem
to show that librarians from several institutions thought no
funds were available (see Table 82). A total of 176 (78. 6%)
of the librarians, as compared with a considerably larger
number, 191 (93. 2%), of the faculty members, said that they
were aware of the availability of funds for special research
projects. Possibly part of the difference can be explained
on the basis of lack of interest, or failure to inquire, or
negligence on the part of the chief librarian in informing his
staff. But it would also seem to point to unequal opportunity, and a number of librarians made special note of the
fact that such support was available to the faculty but not to
librarians. Thus discrimination against librarians may account partially for the fact that only eight (3. 6%) of them requested funds whereas 41 (20%) or one of every five faculty
members did so (see Tables 83 and 84).

Six of eight (75%) of the librarians who applied for
funds received them, whereas 37 of 41 (90. 2%) of the faculty
members were successful in getting assistance. The difference is statistically significant above the . 001 level.

Presumably, granting time to librarians for research
projects is more directly within the province of the director
of libraries. Still, only three (1. 3%) of the librarians received time, but 18 (8. 8%) of the faculty had that benefit.

TABLE 82

Knowledge of Availability of Research Funds

| | Librarians | | Faculty | |
	No.	%	No.	%
Yes	176	78. 6	191	93. 2
No	45	20. 1	11	5. 4
Do not know	3	1. 3	3	1. 4
Total	224	100. 0	205	100. 0

TABLE 83

Research Funds and Time for Research Requested
and Received by Librarians by Sex

| | Men | | Women | | Total | |
	No.	%	No.	%	No.	%
Requested funds						
Yes	6	5. 3	2	1. 8	8	3. 6
No	101	89. 4	108	97. 3	209	93. 3
No response	6	5. 3	1	0. 9	7	3. 1
Total	113	100. 0	111	100. 0	224	100. 0
Received funds						
Yes	4	3. 5	2	1. 8	6	2. 7
No	101	89. 4	106	95. 5	207	92. 4
No response	8	7. 1	3	2. 7	11	4. 9
Total	113	100. 0	111	100. 0	224	100. 0
Received time						
Yes	0	0. 0	3	2. 7	3	1. 3
No	111	98. 2	107	96. 4	218	97. 4
No response	2	1. 8	1	0. 9	3	1. 3
Total	113	100. 0	111	100. 0	224	100. 0

TABLE 84

Research Funds and Time for Research Requested
and Received by Faculty Members by Sex

	Men		Women		Total	
	No.	%	No.	%	No.	%
Requested funds						
Yes	37	22. 8	4	9. 3	41	20. 0
No	121	74. 7	38	88. 4	159	77. 6
No response	4	2. 5	1	2. 3	5	2. 4
Total	162	100. 0	43	100. 0	205	100. 0
Received funds						
Yes	34	21. 0	3	7. 0	37	18. 1
No	122	75. 3	38	88. 3	160	78. 0
No response	6	3. 7	2	4. 7	8	3. 9
Total	162	100. 0	43	100. 0	205	100. 0
Received time						
Yes	16	9. 9	2	4. 7	18	8. 8
No	141	87. 0	41	95. 3	182	88. 8
No response	5	3. 1	0	0. 0	5	2. 4
Total	162	100. 0	43	100. 0	205	100. 0

TABLE 85

Research Funds Received by
Librarians and Faculty Members

	Librarians	Faculty
Received funds	6	37
Did not receive funds	207	160
x^2 28. 3 df 1 P . 001		

Travel Funds

As Tables 86 and 87 show, a larger proportion of the librarians (68.8%) than faculty members (60%) received travel funds, and librarians were also more likely to receive expenses. Differences by sex are conspicuous for both groups. Among faculty members and librarians a larger percentage of the men received travel funds. It is worth noting that 13% more of the male librarians (75.2%) received funds and that more received travel plus per diem or full expenses (44.2%) than is the case for the female librarians (62.2% and 28.9% respectively). Thus the male librarians have a distinct advantage both in the percentage who received funds and in the percentage who received travel plus per diem. In spite of this difference, approximately the same percentage of female librarians (62.2%) received travel funds as did male faculty members (62.4%) who, in turn, still were more likely to receive this benefit than faculty women (51.2%).

TABLE 86

Travel Funds Received by Librarians
by Sex During the Past Year

	Men		Women		Total	
	No.	%	No.	%	No.	%
Received funds	85	75.2	69	62.2	154	68.8
Travel & per diem[a]	50	44.2	32	28.9	82	36.6
Partial[b]	35	31.0	37	33.3	72	32.1
Did not receive funds	24	21.3	41	36.9	65	29.0
No response	4	3.5	1	0.9	5	2.2

[a]Also includes those who reported having received all expenses.

[b]Includes many variations such as travel only, travel plus meals, travel plus registration, a specified sum of money, or as decided by the director of libraries.

TABLE 87

Travel Funds Received by Faculty Members
by Sex During the Past Year

	Men		Women		Total	
	No.	%	No.	%	No.	%
Received funds	101	62. 4	22	51. 2	123	60. 0
Travel & per diem[a]	55	34. 0	11	25. 6	66	32. 2
Partial[b]	46	28. 4	11	25. 6	57	27. 8
Did not receive funds	59	36. 4	20	46. 5	79	38. 5
No response	2	1. 2	1	2. 3	3	1. 5

[a]Also includes those who reported having received all expenses.

[b]Includes many variations such as travel only, travel plus meals, travel plus registration, a specified sum of money, or as decided by the department chairman or dean.

That librarians were more likely to receive funds than faculty members is statistically significant above the . 05 level (see Table 88).

TABLE 88

Travel Funds Received by Librarians and
Faculty Members During the Past Year

	Librarians	Faculty
Received funds	154	123
Did not receive funds	65	79

| x^2 | 4. 1 | df | 1 | P | . 05 |

Chapter 8

Comments by Faculty Members and Librarians

In addition to remarks such as "good luck" and "I'm
glad you're doing this study, " 104 (50. 7%) of the faculty
members and a somewhat smaller number of 93 (41. 5%) of
the librarians made comments ranging from a few sentences
to several pages.   Although a larger percentage of the faculty members took the time to make a statement, the librarians who gave their opinions were more loquacious.   Possibly
this reflects a greater concern with the issues on the part of
the librarians.

Some of the remarks made specific reference to such
questions as access to research funds, tenure, the quality of
library service, or the capabilities of the director of libraries, while others addressed themselves to the broad issue
of faculty status itself.   Since the respondents spent a significant amount of time answering the questionnaire and
writing comments, it seems only fair to permit them to
speak in their own words.   While excerpts are taken from
some statements, others are quoted at length.

Comments by Faculty Members

Seven faculty members stated that the Wisconsin State
Universities have no sabbaticals but rather "teacher-improve-
ment leaves, " and four of the seven said that these were
given mainly to faculty members completing their work for
the doctorate.   Two others, evidently not from Wisconsin,
wrote that they would become eligible for a sabbatical only
if they stayed long enough, and staying depended upon completing the doctorate which was a requirement for tenure.
Only after getting tenure would they actually become eligible
for a sabbatical.

Among those who commented on whether they were
under pressure to pursue the doctorate, several said they
accepted the fact that the doctorate was necessary for a

teaching position in a university, and a few more felt "strong internal pressure." Six stated that they had, or almost had, the degree before accepting a full-time teaching position and therefore felt under no duress.

A comparatively large number, 21, commented on the education of librarians. One said the degree alone should not be the determining factor and another emphasized "learning" rather than academic degrees:

> Librarians and all other members of the academic community are overly concerned with degrees and rank and not professional competence. I would favor the abolishment of degree requirements, tenure, and rank and place job retention upon performance. Many people here have pursued the Ed. D. simply because they had to in order to get more money, and their additional education has nothing to do with their job and has only taken time away from their duties and reduced their effectiveness.

Generally, they tended to stress the need for formal study for members of the library staff:

> Many of the general operational positions should be civil service, or a similar category with varying qualifications according to the specific job. The head librarian and those in other positions with major responsibilities should have at least the master's (probably in both a discipline and in library science) and preferably a doctorate. This group--the more responsible positions-- should have faculty status. The others should not.

Eleven felt they lacked acquaintance with the specific duties of librarians, stated that the degree depends on the position, or did not know what a professional librarian is.

> I don't quite know enough of libraries to distinguish between a 'professional librarian' and the person that files books or checks them out, etc.

> I think the biggest problem that librarians must overcome is that few faculty distinguish between those who work in libraries and librarians. Too often inexperienced or incompetent library help are called 'librarians,' especially when errors are made.

One maintained that there is no such profession as librar-

ianship. Still another said that only the Ed. D. rather than
the Ph. D. should be given in library science because giving
the latter would "tend to degrade the Ph. D. , " which is a
"research degree. " Three stated that rewards such as
salary and tenure should be tied to faculty standards.   As
one put it,

> In order to get any recognition in a department such as
> English one has to have the Doctorate, the same should
> hold true for library personnel--earned Doctorate in li-
> brary science.

Two expressed dissatisfaction with opportunities and
support for research.   One said that funds are available only
for "Mickey Mouse pretentious projects. "   Another said his
institution was still a teachers college in spite of its name
and was not interested in research.

Only one person commented on the question of membership in professional associations, saying, "I am not a
club woman. I am a teacher and a scholar. "   Six expressed
dissatisfaction about the way faculty government operates in
their institutions, and made observations such as:

> The Faculty Senate is a company union, more reactionary
> if possible than the administration.

> I never participate in the elections (held in the dean's
> office).

> Practically speaking only old or campus politicians are
> elected.

> To the best of my knowledge I am eligible for election
> to the faculty senate de jure--but not de facto.

A question that engendered much comment was the one
which asked faculty members to rank ten positions in order
of importance from one to ten.   Evidently, some felt that
even posing the question of whether some positions were
more important than others would serve as a divisive element.   Others either thought that no differences exist, that
it was best not to discuss such issues, or that all were equal.
Accompanying remarks ranged from "this is dirty, " or "This
is a loaded question" and "This is unfair, " to "I don't know
them well enough" or "This question is very difficult to
answer, " or "I refuse to do so.   They have different func-

tions" and "I consider them all equal." One respondent who
put librarians in the number one position added, "Sorry about
that ranking, but I feel that way." One did not know what
instructional media personnel are, and another asked whether
there was any difference between instructional media personnel and librarians.

That librarians are not the only ones who experience
opposition is shown by the fact that five faculty members expressed dismay at the practice of changing the library to an
instructional media center which, according to them, reflected
an interest in gadgets. As one respondent wrote:

> We seem to have a thing about electronics. We are weak
> in library volumes, but strong in gimmicks like 'random
> access' and 'dial-a-tape.' Unfortunately these don't
> seem to work. The library itself is lowest on the ladder
> in terms of attention given it by the administration.

Another writer thought that the "educationists who splice film
are regrettably equated with librarians."

Only three faculty members felt it necessary to make
a statement on the importance of the faculty in the academic
community with views such as "I think the faculty is the
most important in any university" and "I do not think that librarians and faculty members should have the same status"
and a thoughtful statement:

> I am a little doubtful whether librarians should be con-
> sidered teaching faculty, especially as many of the po-
> sitions are administrative. Still they are not adminis-
> trators. Since the positions and tasks are different (be-
> tween librarians and faculty) are similar rewards appro-
> priate or even desirable?

> This question occurs despite a belief that librarians need
> better conditions, higher status, and more influence in
> order to improve college libraries to the fullest possible
> extent.

A small number denigrated the library staff at their
institutions. One called the entire staff "incompetent except
for the top one or two positions," and another felt that librarians were

> notably deficient in general education. I fail to see why

it is a 'profession' to order and file a book, other than
the well-known American propensity for high-sounding
titles.

One faculty member affirmed categorically, "In many libraries I know more about the library than the librarians.   I
have a doctorate in literature. " However, several placed
most of the blame on the chief librarian, who in many institutions has considerable impact on how the faculty judges librarians.

> There is less staff participation and more domination by
> the director of libraries than in any other department on
> the campus.

> The major problems here with library-faculty relation-
> ships seems to stem from a highly autocratic head li-
> brarian who is both unwilling and unable to explain li-
> brary problems.   Furthermore, he resists any attempt
> to investigate the whole library operation, which he views
> as his personal bailiwick.   Employees considered guilty
> of a breach of 'security' find themselves in an intoler-
> able situation and quit, much to his satisfaction.

> They [the librarians] elect their own representative to
> the faculty senate (always the director, who else?) who
> invariably votes with the administration.   Our faculty
> senate is loaded with deans, librarians, directors of
> student activities, and deans of students, and we, the
> teaching faculty, are totally disgusted with it.

Three felt that librarians were status seekers in trying to
gain equality with the faculty.   Giving fatherly advice, one
of these wrote,

> I recommend good will, open ears, hard work with high
> standards, a thoughtful reading of Vance Packard's Status
> Seekers, being part of the solution instead of part of the
> problem, talking less about money and more about
> service.

> What kind of 'recognition' do librarians seek?   Money?
> Rank?   Voting power?   I like to say thank you, but to
> whom?   Where and when?

> It has been my experience that malcontents usually pro-
> duce their own conditions of unhappiness--?

Most of the faculty members had high praise for librarians.
Some felt that the librarians at their institution had won
great respect from the faculty and were regularly elected
to important faculty committees.

> The head librarian is a truly learned man, alert and
> hard-working, who is doing wonderful work under diffi-
> cult conditions.

> The head librarian is an active, volatile, effective par-
> ticipant in all faculty affairs.

> Our library staff is excellent.

> I rank the librarians right at the top.

> They [the librarians] are informed, helpful people, and
> they promote an atmosphere of service and free inquiry
> that equals any fostered by the faculty.

> Pompous faculty egoists who regard librarians as clerks
> win my unmitigated scorn.

> An able and dedicated library staff such as ours is one
> of the most important assets a college can acquire.

> It is my impression that librarians are not sufficiently
> appreciated in most university campuses and that, in-
> deed, their rights and privileges are incommensurate
> with their responsibilities.

> Our college has an excellent, fully professional, badly
> overworked library staff with full faculty status.   Three
> of the staff are, for example, members of AAUP and
> one is vice-president and president elect (and a past
> president) of AAUP.

Only three faculty members expressed displeasure
with the questionnaire itself.

> This is a rather meaningless questionnaire and one
> would hope that more substantive projects would be
> available for Ph. D. research.

> I can't see the merit of the questions you ask, but sup-
> pose you have a reason for each one.

> This question [the last item] turned me off concerning
> your entire effort. Are you concerned only with status?
> Does cooperation to do a job have no meaning?

The latter respondent refused to complete the questionnaire
and was not counted as one of the 205 which were analyzed.

Comments by Librarians

Although most of the librarians in the survey have
faculty status, the battle has not necessarily been won for
all time. Two head librarians and five others expressed
apprehension about the possibility that librarians in their institution might lose this advantage. Furthermore, while
several wrote that they thought academic year contracts were
the most important benefit of faculty status, two said that the
administration at their institution was trying to coerce librarians into accepting 12-month contracts. One of the most
adamant comments on faculty status for librarians was:

> The day they drop librarians from faculty status, if and
> when they ever do, I will return to the Public Schools
> as a School Librarian.

Only two took exception to the idea of faculty status
for librarians. One of the dissenters wrote,

> I do not see how librarians deserve academic rank and
> title (or for that matter how any administrative position
> such as 'Dean of this or that' deserves it), since my
> idea of faculty means either teaching or scholarly re-
> search. Librarians are certainly essential, but faculty
> they are not--faculty teach, librarians assist them. Li-
> brarians are technicians, not scholars. A librarian may
> also be a scholar, of course (or a poet or a motorcycle
> racer) but his scholarly activities are no gauge of his
> abilities as a librarian.... Let us take pride in what
> we do, and do it well, and stop all this vain (in both
> senses of the word) striving for social recognition.

At greater length the other dissenter raised the question of
whether tasks performed by librarians are of a professional
nature. She also thought the master's degree was most adequate unless she were given more challenging duties.

I thought at one time faculty status was important and

something to be sought after, but I am not sure I think
that anymore.   I question whether it is desirable or even
possible.   A recent recommendation was made at our
university where librarians have faculty status, '... that
a nine-hour teaching load be the normal practice, so
that each staff member might devote time to research,
publications, curriculum and personal professional improvement.'   How this would be interpreted in regard to
librarians who work from 8 - 5 and therefore lack the
flexible schedules of teaching faculty should prove interesting and challenging.   Frequently my work (circulation and periodicals) is more administrative and clerical than academic.   Unless I should move to a larger
university and engage in another phase of library work,
I would not consider earning another degree in a subject
speciality, since I would not have an opportunity to make
use of my new knowledge in my present position.

Faculty (librarians) with all the markings of civil service
are thought of and treated as civil service.   Better for
the librarians if their work and training is recognized
for what it is, their own special position is established
in the university separated from faculty, administration
and classified civil service.

A number of other respondents broached the question
of professional and non-professional tasks in a different
fashion by insisting that those who perform only routine tasks
should not be considered librarians.   One, for example, felt
that

We all have a long way to go in achieving full faculty
status, but we will not necessarily do it without changing many of the ways in which we have been doing
things.   We can say 'It is not our fault that we have
been burdened by clerical routines: The work HAD to be
done and the administration could not give us the clerical
personnel to do it.'   But we have in fact let ourselves
get all cluttered up with clerical junk.   We must be doing two things at once: We must be forging toward faculty status for all professional librarians despite little
people who have gotten onto professional library staffs
by default; at the same time we must be cleaning out our
house by separating those many tasks which are merely
supervisory and high-level clerical, giving these tasks
to paraprofessional staff with college degrees and, perhaps, a few courses in library science, and call by the

term librarians only those fully academic, fully faculty
personnel about whom there will be no question of faculty
status. If we think we can have little ladies who knit
for a hobby and check in serials all day long for faculty
status library staff members, then we are groping for
what cannot be had. If we cannot separate much of the
inter-library loan work, circulation work, routine pro-
cedural supervision work (e. g. , mechanical preparation
of materials, bindery preparation, stack collection housekeeping work--all of which a bright guy with a college
degree and a desire to do things right can handle well),
and a lot of other things off into the 'middle service'
or paraprofessional or whatever we want to call it, then
we are stupid to think that we are going to gain 'faculty
status. '

     One librarian thought too much emphasis was placed
on degrees.

Service to faculty and students is what brings recognition
to library personnel! There is entirely too much emphasis on work-beyond-the-etc. and not enough on serv-
ice-at-the-here-and-now-level.

It is a sad commentary on our sense of values to see
that a few staff members are extolled for constantly
'taking courses' when these same few are also 'taking
time' (stealing time would 'tell it like it is') from their
duties to do the course assignments. For those people
their sense of service is to themselves, not to their
constituents! These are usually the success-ridden
young people who even just out of school continue on
toward further degrees, but who cannot find a book for
themselves even in their own libraries!

One may have a doctorate in ichthyology or paleontology,
but if he cannot help a patron find a subject heading to
cover his interest, his patron will walk away with the
conviction, further entrenched, that librarians are
'stupid. '

'In-service' training is a misnomer--for too often the
in-service trainee is 'out-of-service' on the job.

Sabbatical leaves and leaves of absences are most certainly a more honest and efficient approach to further
study; the only draw-backs are that in the case of sab-

baticals in any sizeable institution there are many more
applicants than there is money.   In the case of annual
leaves--many cannot afford to take the time off without
pay and spend the money to go to school besides.   However, often these people are much more knowledgeable
and worthy 'on the job' than the avid increment seeker.

Another thought that the master's degree should be the educational requirement with promotion based on longevity.

Not believing that it is necessary to go beyond the M. S.
in the average library position, I think raises in faculty
rank should be automatically based on longevity.   Perhaps assistant professor 7 years, associate professor
15 years, professor 25 years.   I also feel something
should be done to compensate librarians for their 40
hour (including nights and weekends) work week in comparison with what faculty receive for meeting occasional
classes.

Others stressed the need for continuing education and meeting faculty standards.

It seems to me that librarians in the Wisconsin State
University system are somewhat ahead of the national
average in terms of faculty status and benefits.   Cor-
respondingly, full faculty obligations for tenure and promotion must be met.   The pressure for additional
credits and/or degrees is constant for any librarian remaining in this state system.   All in all, a fair and
equitable expectation.

It is my strong belief that librarians employed in colleges or universities, who wish faculty status identical
with that of 'teaching' faculty, must accept identical educational schedules.   We are a minority of the total
faculty.   When we protest applicability of that schedule
to librarians, I think it not strange if 'teaching' faculty
respond by questioning if we really belong in their group.

A few commented specifically on degree requirements and
pressure to work toward the doctorate:

There is no pressure as long as one is willing to remain at the same academic rank.   For promotions in
rank one must work toward a doctorate.   For those who
have started to work here later than I did progress

toward a doctorate is tied in with tenure. The policy
really is not clear as far as librarians are concerned;
to date no librarians have been dismissed because they
have not worked toward a doctorate, but the fact that
there is a 'substantial progress' policy hangs heavy over
our heads. This policy is set by the University Administrators, not the Director of Libraries.

When I first came here, there was no mention or pressure about my doing advanced work (Fall, 1963). Present practice is to inform new people that such work is
expected, or tenure can't be expected. What with the
supply/demand situation of librarians, it remains to be
seen if this stipulation will be enforced.

I feel no pressure to work toward the Ph. D., but there
is a definite self-interest to be served by obtaining work
beyond your master's degree since rank depends upon it.

Four more stated that promotion and tenure were contingent
upon "substantial progress" toward the doctorate but that the
second master's was not considered acceptable in place of
the doctorate for librarians:

I've been on a committee within our library to make a
recommendation to the University administration concerning the appropriate terminal degree for librarians. This
is of importance here because tenure hinges on progress
on or attainment of the terminal degree. Our recommendation as I've answered on this questionnaire is the
fifth-year professional degree. This is not to be taken
though as the end. Subject degrees and advanced library
degrees do have their place which our committee will in-
corporate into our recommendations to the administration
concerning promotion in rank. Recently, the Regents of
our system have ruled that second master's degrees will
not count for promotion. We hope to have an exception
made for librarians.

One respondent reported that the recent arrival of a
new director of libraries had a marked impact on the attitude
of the staff and that the librarians were receptive to the director's emphasis on participation in professional activities
and further education.

Four participants in the survey felt that faculty status
had no value unless it insured equal benefits, and in some

instances the percentages of yes or no responses do not tell
the complete story. With regard to sabbaticals, for example,
three librarians reported that they were "supposedly" or
"technically" eligible but that at their institution no librarian
who had applied had ever received one. Thus being eligible
is of no significance if requests are still denied. What applies to sabbaticals also pertains to other benefits of faculty
status such as tenure and access to research funds, for
several librarians stated that these were rarely given to librarians at their institution.

> A library or university administration can say in theory
> a librarian has all these privileges whereas in reality
> leaves of absences etc. might never be granted. Also
> a library administrator can pursue a policy of never
> granting tenure or to very few, so that in reality one is
> never eligible.

Naturally institutions differ in policies, and a library director
was pleased to report that within the last few years two librarians had applied for teacher improvement leaves with
half salary and both had received them.

> Eleven specifically noted the responsibilities of faculty
status.

> Because of the market place, we tend to get lower sala-
> ries than faculty in the sciences particularly, and our
> prestige is not high. But this is partly or mostly our
> own fault, as none of the 7 librarians here have a doc-
> torate or publish anything of any significance. In fact,
> I'm not sure anyone has published anything. So we can't
> complain if those faculty who do have advanced degrees
> and publications don't consider us scholarly.

> Librarians have always been insistent about a clear de-
> finition of their status in the academic community. The
> ACRL resolution is merely a re-iteration of a 'voice in
> the wilderness.' This would not be true if librarians
> held the same insistence that advanced study, scholarly
> writing, service to the University, was equal to that of
> the teaching faculty, in terms of actual participation.
> There has never been any hesitance on the part of the
> faculty at this University to recognize me as their peer.
> I owe this to the fact that I have volunteered my services
> to the total University mission; not to just empire build-
> ing in a remote corner of the library. Not only have I

been elected to the position of President of the University Faculty Senate, but I have also served on many
other committees.... In summary, we cannot demand
equal status by means of mere resolution. WE MUST
EARN OUR STATUS AND PEER ACCEPTANCE IN THE
ACADEMIC COMMUNITY.

That the question of the appropriate educational requirement for librarians is still an unresolved issue is indicated by the fact that 47 librarians commented on the item
asking about the appropriate minimal and terminal degrees
for librarians. Most of them maintained that the educational
qualifications must be determined on the basis of the position
itself, and virtually all of the points of view advanced in the
literature can be found in the comments. Respondents argued
for less library science or for more. They recommended
the sixth-year master's degree or the specialist certificate
in library science; more subject specialization; a clearer
delineation of professional work before raising the issue of
degrees; the master's in library science as a minimal degree but then course work in many disciplines rather than
degrees; more emphasis on instructional media; against
terminal degrees for anyone, especially librarians, etc.
Nevertheless, in spite of the divergent points of view, the
majority favored the master's in library science as the minimal degree. For the terminal degree no majority viewpoint
exists; the master's in library science, the sixth-year specialist degree, the second master's in another subject, and
the doctorate, whether in library science or in another subject, all have their passionate advocates.

The items asking librarians how they thought the faculty would rank them and how they would rank themselves
generated 43 comments, a response second only to that on
the appropriate degrees for librarians. Favoring egalitar-
ianism, some felt that it was not a matter of ranking the
positions from one to ten but rather from one to three or
four. Because 43 (19.2%) of the respondents refused to
commit themselves on the question of how they thought the
faculty would rank librarians at their institution, and 34
(15.2%) failed to indicate how they thought librarians should
rank, it is worth quoting some of the observations on these
items.

Even janitors rank higher than librarians.

This is very subjective; [it] depends upon the individual

faculty member and the librarian concerned.

[There is] too much intrigue, too many unknowns.

I have not been here long enough to know.

Outside of the academic dean, I believe they are pretty much the same.

Several are equal. I would use 2 numbers, academic dean 1, all others 2.

I don't think enough of the faculty would agree enough so one could answer for the <u>faculty</u>. I think each group is apt to consider <u>itself</u> the most important. I think they are equally important, if each does well the job he is supposed to be doing, for the welfare of the whole university community.

The library director ought to rank just under the academic dean, surely; but that does not say that a brand new junior reference librarian ought to.

I really do not think prestige is a factor.

Prestige depends upon the person filling the position.

I think of all faculty (everyone but administrators) as equal in prestige, administrators as higher.

The ranking in this question is probably pure conjecture; with close to 500 faculty members I feel it is impossible to draw conclusions based on the entire faculty. I have attempted to answer based on the small percentage of faculty members I have known or been able to observe.

Since 22. 8% of the librarians had been at their present institution for less than a year and since 10. 7% had less than a year of experience as academic librarians, it is understandable why many of them pleaded lack of acquaintance with the faculty and therefore did not respond to this item. On the other hand, one might expect most if not all of them to have an opinion on how librarians should rank among the ten positions.

Summary

As far as faculty status for librarians is concerned, the most significant comments pertained to the education and scholarly activities of librarians. Although a few respondents felt too much emphasis was placed on degrees, most of them agreed that librarians should have identical or at least similar education to that expected of the faculty. It is worthy of note that the major criticisms faculty members leveled against librarians involved: (1) the librarians' lack of education; (2) the conviction that librarianship as a discipline is not worthy of study; and (3) the inadequacies of the head librarian who is either dictatorial or inept or both. Few faculty members made comments which were critical of librarians. More praised librarians because: (1) the head librarian is an intelligent, effective participant in academic affairs; and (2) librarians are well-informed people who create an atmosphere of free inquiry. Thus both the areas of praise and blame involve the intellectual attainment of librarians and the director's qualifications and method of operation. A few faculty members held a stereotyped view of the media specialist as someone who "splices film."

Nearly all of the librarians have faculty status, but a number of them fear losing it. Only two librarians questioned the appropriateness of close identification between librarians and faculty members, and both wondered whether librarians deserved faculty status because of the tasks they perform and because they do not engage in scholarly activity. Pressure upon librarians to pursue additional graduate work in some instances is coming from institutional criteria for appointment, promotion, and tenure. "Substantial progress" toward the doctorate is a requirement for gaining tenure in some institutions, and the second master's degree is not considered an acceptable substitute.

Several librarians stated that they were theoretically but not actually eligible for sabbaticals, research funds, and tenure.

Some librarians felt that they did not know the faculty well enough to judge how the faculty at their institution would rank librarians, and others thought all of the ten positions should be ranked either one or two or from one to three or four rather than from one to ten. Some of the faculty respondents believed that the question of how the various positions should rank should not be broached or that all were equal or nearly so.

Chapter 9

General Summary and Conclusions

Part I of this study contains an examination of the literature pertaining to the struggle of academic librarians to gain faculty status in colleges and universities in the United States. Not intended as an exhaustive review, this discussion cites various points of view regarding both the responsibilities and benefits of faculty status. Part II consists of a discussion of the findings of a survey conducted in the fall of 1969. This last chapter is a brief summary of the literature and the survey, with conclusions based on both Parts I and II of this study.

Summary: Related Literature

Status for an individual may be defined as the relative position he holds within a society or an organization, and a profession is also accorded a position within the society's prestige structure. Although the status of a profession depends upon how society values the service performed by the practitioners, its prestige is also closely and consistently related to the amount of education required for that occupation. The academic librarian seeks status in the college or university, but no universally accepted definition of faculty status or academic status exists. Sometimes academic status and faculty status have been used interchangeably, although academic status has usually meant that librarians were members of the instructional and research staff whereas faculty status also included academic rank.

As defined in this study, faculty status includes academic rank and titles and equal treatment with the faculty in matters such as: (1) salaries; (2) voting privileges in the institution's governing body; (3) vacations; (4) sabbaticals and other leaves; (5) access to research and travel funds; (6) tenure; and (7) service on faculty committees.

Although it is sometimes difficult to assess the re-

sults of previous surveys because writers failed to define
terms, it is clear that librarians have increasingly gained
acceptance as members of the academic staff and, in fewer
instances, as full-fledged members of the faculty. Still,
some librarians maintain that few of them are treated equally
with the faculty in matters of salary, vacations, tenure, sabbaticals, access to research funds, etc.

Librarians themselves have not agreed upon what kind
of status they should have. They have made recommendations
which include full faculty status, equivalent rank, identification as academic but without reference to faculty rank, a
separate classification, and classification with administrative
officers. Motivations for seeking an improved status may
reflect a pursuit of status for its own sake, a desire for
social acceptance, a conviction that faculty status increases
the librarian's opportunity to be of service, or a concern for
improved salaries and other benefits.

Many librarians have stressed the view that the practitioners, if they want faculty status, must meet the educational standards of the faculty; others maintain that librarians
are not receiving adequate rewards for the qualifications they
already possess. That their educational level has risen in
the past 50 or 60 years is evident from the surveys on this
topic. The early studies show that many librarians did not
have the bachelor's degree, but the vast majority of academic
librarians in recent surveys have at least a master's degree
and many have additional graduate degrees. Except for the
top administrative levels in the larger institutions, only a
small percentage of the librarians have the doctorate, but
about 40% to 60% of the faculty members in various types of
institutions have that degree.

Because criteria for faculty appointment often included
possession of the doctorate, some writers have suggested
that librarians should also have that degree; others say librarians do not need it. Generally the professionals have
urged the utility of a second or third master's degree. Because additional educational preparation is considered desirable for practitioners, incentive systems could contribute
substantially to staff development; but at least one writer has
suggested that the best incentive for staff development is to
give greater responsibilities to the staff. If they are given
challenging tasks, librarians, according to this view, are
more likely to seek the formal and informal education they
need.

As with education, the academic community has a high regard for research and publication. While some argue the need to devote more time and energy to these endeavors, other writers believe that librarians should not be expected to engage in such activities as extensively as does the faculty. According to most accounts, rigid work schedules are a deterrent to scholarly activity on the part of librarians, and library administrators feel that those who are interested should invest substantially of their own time.

To some librarians, serving on academic committees is an indication of acceptance by the faculty and central administration. Librarians seem to be more insistent about participation in academic affairs and to engage in them more extensively now than they did 20 or 30 years ago. At the same time librarians emphasize participation in the activities of professional associations.

Many writers have commented on the fact that librarianship for many years has been a feminine profession. In the top administrative positions in the larger institutions men predominate. The smaller the college or university, the greater the likelihood that the head librarian will be a woman, and a large proportion of the professional staff in most academic libraries tends to be female. According to the literature, this would seem to have certain implications for academic librarianship. Because many women leave the labor force for a number of years when their children are young, the majority of the female librarians are either younger or older than the majority of the male faculty members. Then too, a smaller percentage of women earn the doctorate, they devote less time and energy to research and publication, they are to some extent victims of both self-imposed and unwarranted discrimination, they are less mobile (which makes them less competitive for salaries and positions), they tend to be less self-assertive, and they are less likely to be concerned about status and salaries.

Traditionally, writers on library administration have proposed that faculty rank should be related to the position held; that is, the head librarian should be a professor or dean, the associate librarian an associate professor, and department heads assistant professors. For the faculty, academic rank has depended upon factors such as degrees, scholarly activity, teaching ability, professional activity, and general contributions to the institution. Recently, some practitioners have suggested that the academic rank of librarians should be determined on the basis of their background, abilities, and contributions, in a fashion similar to that used for faculty members, without regard to their administrative position.

Whatever the procedures used for determining it, academic rank for librarians raises the question of qualifications. In many colleges and universities the doctorate may be a criterion for promotion; and in the larger universities the degree as well as evidence of scholarship, professional activity, and service to the institution may be involved. To some writers it becomes a matter, then, of whether librarians meet the standards of appointment and promotion which are used for the faculty.

If the librarians are to meet faculty standards, being eligible for sabbatical leaves is an important benefit, but previous surveys suggest that librarians do not receive equal treatment in this area.

While salaries have been a perennial concern, librarians generally have not made a concerted drive to improve their remuneration. To some writers, the level of compensation is a measure of the value the institution places on the library staff. Most of the surveyors have concluded that the remuneration of librarians is lower than that of faculty members, but few of the surveys have explicitly compared faculty members and librarians with regard to salaries, rank, education, scholarly activity, and contributions to the institution and the profession. Since having the doctorate is related both to academic rank and to salaries within each rank, the degree itself is an important consideration in judging equitable compensation.

Comparatively little attention has been paid to tenure for academic librarians, and some library administrators hold that it has little or no application to librarians. Efforts have been made recently to encourage greater staff participation in library management. If this becomes a trend, librarians will probably become more concerned about tenure.

While travel funds are inadequate in many libraries, the literature suggests that academic librarians are usually as well off as faculty members in this regard. One writer maintains that funds are not the critical issue. If the program is of high quality and if the librarian thinks he will be exposed to new ideas which apply to his work, he is likely to attend professional meetings.

Summary: The Survey

In the present survey questionnaires were sent to 281
librarians and 339 faculty members; 224 (79. 9%) librarians
and 205 (60. 5%) faculty members responded in time for analysis.   The faculty subjects were a 20% random sample of
full-time teachers from the departments of biology, economics, English, history, physics, and sociology.   All of
the full-time librarians employed in the 19 institutions were
included.   Of the 429 replies, 52. 2% were from librarians
and 47. 8% from teaching faculty.   Among the librarians, 113,
or slightly more than half (50. 4%), were men and 111 (49. 6%)
were women.   The faculty totals consisted of 162 men (79%)
and 43 women (21%).

For the librarians the average age was 40. 9 years and
for the faculty it was 39. 8.   More than one of every five librarians has joined the staff at his present institution within
the past year.   This applies to approximately one of every
20 faculty members.   More than 40% of the total sample have
had five or fewer years of experience.   Over 70% of the
sample have been at their present institution for five years
or fewer.

Nearly all of the librarians have at least the master's
degree, and many have two master's, the sixth-year degree,
or the doctorate.   A majority of the librarians set the
master's degree as the minimal preparation for academic librarians.   As for the terminal degree, less consistency
exists.   The master's in library science is still first choice,
but many respondents recommend two master's degrees or
the doctorate, and some gave a qualified answer saying that
no degree should be terminal or that the educational requirements depend upon the position held.

Nearly two-thirds of the librarians have earned credits
beyond their highest degrees.   The average number of semester credit hours earned is 16. 1.   A minority feel pressure to work toward the doctorate.   While 71 (31. 7%) expect
to earn another degree, 30 (13. 4%) have set the doctorate as
their goal.   A total of 42 (18. 8%) either have or hope to earn
the doctorate, which approximates the number, 44 (19. 6%),
who recommend the doctorate as the appropriate terminal degree.   This may suggest that librarians set the standards of

education on the basis of their own attainments and aspirations and that as the percentage of librarians with the doctorate increases more emphasis may be put on that degree.

Among the faculty over half have the doctorate.   All
but one of the others have the master's degree.   Those who
do not have the doctorate have earned an average of 30. 9
semester credits beyond their highest degree, and the majority of them expect to earn the doctorate.   Nearly three-
quarters of the faculty members feel (or felt) pressure to
earn the doctorate.

While more faculty members than librarians recommended the bachelor's as the basic professional degree, over
half of them suggested the master's degree.   For the terminal degree, over half of the faculty members deemed the
doctorate most appropriate.   Few of them urged the second
master's degree.   In general, then, the faculty members
have more formal education, higher educational aspirations,
feel (or felt) under greater pressure to work toward the doctorate, and more of them recommend the doctorate as the
appropriate terminal degree for librarians.   The differences
between the faculty members and librarians regarding educational attainment, aspirations, and pressure to work toward
the doctorate were statistically significant above the . 01
level.   Taken as a group, the head librarians have more
formal education than the other librarians, but the head librarians on the average have less formal education than the
faculty members.

Faculty members were more likely to publish than librarians (statistically significant above the . 001 level).   Both
among librarians and faculty members, those with the doctorate published more than those without that degree.   On the
average, the male head librarians published more than the
male faculty members, but the female head librarians reported no publications.

Except for those librarians who do not have faculty
rank, virtually all of the librarians are voting members of
the faculty and a larger percentage of the librarians reported
being members of the faculty senate than did the faculty respondents.   The faculty members were on more committees.
For librarians, service on academic committees is related
to the position held; a larger percentage of the head librarians and of those in other administrative positions served on
committees.   Not having faculty rank did not preclude mem-

bership on academic committees.

Faculty members average more memberships in national associations, but librarians hold more in state associations.

Among the librarians, 208 (92. 9%) have faculty rank and titles. While a few librarians were fearful of losing it, only two questioned the desirability of faculty status for librarians.

Five of the librarians have no academic rank or titles, six have equivalent rank, and five are faculty assistants or assistant instructors. Not having academic rank seems to be a critical consideration, for none of the five without it reported being eligible for tenure or sabbaticals. Their salaries were lower, and only the head librarian was a voting member of the faculty. On the other hand, all but one were eligible for service on academic committees. Those with equivalent rank are in general similar to those with faculty rank. Among the faculty an increasing percentage of those in each higher rank has the doctorate. While having the doctorate is not essential for librarians to be promoted to the higher ranks, the fact that few librarians have the doctorate probably accounts for their sparse representation in the higher academic ranks.

Only a small percentage of either faculty members or librarians have received sabbatical leaves. This would seem to indicate a shortage of funds to support the program, but a large proportion of the respondents have been at their present institution or on the staff of a college or university for so short a time that they have never been eligible for the traditional sabbatical leave which normally requires six years of service. Nearly the same percentage of librarians and faculty members are eligible for sabbaticals. More than twice as many librarians and faculty members have taken leaves without pay as have received leaves with pay. Differences between librarians and faculty members in sabbatical leaves received, eligibility for sabbaticals, and leaves of absences taken were not statistically significant.

On the average, respondents with the doctorate earn substantially more than those without it. Those who published also earn more than those who did not, but having published gave less of a salary advantage than having the doctorate.

When taken as a group, librarians earn less than faculty members; but when education is considered, librarians earn approximately the same and in certain cases slightly more than faculty members. The librarians with two master's or the sixth-year degree, for example, on the average earn more than the faculty members with only the master's degree. That these librarians earn more was statistically significant above the .01 level. The faculty members with the master's as the highest degree have earned an average of an additional 30.9 semester hours credits, which is roughly equivalent to the course requirements for a second master's degree or for the sixth-year certificate. When compared with librarians who have only the master's degree, the faculty members with that degree earn more (P   .01).

Although the literature suggests that the 12-month appointment is a hindrance to study toward advanced degrees and scholarly activity, a larger percentage of the librarians in the survey who were on 12-month contracts published (P   .50), and they were as likely to anticipate earning advanced degrees (P   .30). Librarians were less likely than faculty members to receive research funds (P   .001) or time for research and writing. On the other hand, librarians were more likely to receive travel funds than were faculty members (P   .05).

The comments of both faculty members and librarians show that educational level primarily, and to a lesser extent scholarly activity, are related to the prestige of librarians in these institutions. In some colleges and universities criteria for promotion and tenure include "substantial progress" toward the doctorate, and the second master's degree is not an acceptable substitute. Thus the institutions themselves are putting pressure on librarians to pursue advanced study. Except for the five who do not have academic rank, the librarians are eligible for tenure on the same basis as faculty members (P   .90). In some cases librarians appear to be eligible on a more favorable basis than faculty members. In some institutions faculty members must have the doctorate to become eligible for tenure. This does not seem to apply to the librarians.

Although not intended as a sophisticated measure of the librarians' status, one question asked librarians and faculty members to rank ten academic positions including librarians and faculty members in order of importance from 1 (most) to 10 (least). While the librarians thought the faculty would rank them in the number 7 position, the faculty actually ranked librarians in the number 4 position, below only the academic dean, the college of arts and science faculty, and the school of education faculty. This is the same relative position which librarians think they should have.

Variations related to the sex of the respondents were not originally intended as a topic for investigation, but it became evident upon examining the data that for certain questions, differences between male and female librarians were as great as or greater than differences between male librarians and male faculty members. For the total sample and for both the librarian and the faculty as separate groups, educational differences between men and women are conspicuous. The men tend to have both more and higher degrees, and those men who do not have the doctorate have earned more credits beyond their highest degree.

During the past two years the men in the sample published more than the women. The women librarians as a group were well below the average of the female faculty members, the male librarians, and the male faculty members. While less productive than the male faculty member, the average male librarian published more than the average female faculty member. On the average, the male head librarians and the male librarians with the doctorate were more productive in publishing than any other group. The female head librarians reported no publications.

A smaller proportion of the female librarians is in the 31 to 50 age span than is true for either the male librarians or the male faculty members. Thus female librarians tend to be either older or younger than the male librarians and faculty members.

A preliminary inspection of the results suggests women receive unequal treatment in rank and salaries. The average female librarian is below the female faculty member, the male librarian, and the male faculty member in academic rank and in salary. It is important to note, however, that the female librarians are substantially lower in both education and publication and these factors are undoubtedly serious handicaps to advancement. Furthermore, many of the faculty women have been at their institution for a short period of time, and this, together with scholarly activity, undoubtedly has consequences regarding rank.

Faculty men were more likely to receive sabbatical leaves than any other group. Next were male librarians, followed by female librarians and then female faculty members. Because only a small portion of the entire sample (33 of the total 429 respondents) have had a sabbatical, this has not been a major benefit to any group.

Conclusions

Certainly the results of the present survey do not apply to all librarians, but they do have implications for the profession. Some librarians may take issue with the findings reported in this study. Errors of fact deserve note and should be corrected. However, if the reader is distressed by or disagrees with the facts because the facts contradict his personal point of view or his estimate of how he would like things to be, his finding fault with the content is of questionable validity.

Much of the literature in this area would have to be characterized as something less than scholarly, for it often, unfortunately, ignores vital aspects of the question. Although librarians have often been accused of undue concern with minutiae, they can hardly be accused of that with regard to the issue of faculty status. Examples are not hard to find. While many articles cite one or two earlier surveys or expressions of opinion, surprisingly, no previous study has made an extensive examination of the literature on faculty status. Furthermore, after years of discussions regarding faculty and academic status, librarians still have not agreed upon a definition of terms. Hopefully, the 1969 ACRL resolution quoted at the beginning of this study will eventually be accepted as the measure.

Although the present study was not intended as an exhaustive review of the literature, an effort was made to cite viewpoints both from library literature and from other disciplines in order to lend perspective to the examination of both the benefits and the responsibilities of faculty status for librarians.

All the benefits of faculty status included in the definition used in this investigation have received attention in the literature; and many writers have stated that if they want the benefits of faculty status, librarians must be willing to meet faculty standards for appointments, promotion, and tenure.

However the previous surveys have ordinarily sought mainly
to determine whether librarians receive the benefits of faculty status. The investigators have tended to conclude that
librarians received less favorable treatment than the faculty.
The inquiries have usually not asked whether librarians met
faculty criteria in such critical areas as education, research
and writing, service on academic committees, and participation in professional activities. Similarly, in discussing such
vital matters as academic rank, sabbaticals and other leaves,
salaries, and tenure, for example, the discussions in library
literature have paid comparatively little attention to writings
in other disciplines.

The present study is not directly concerned with library management, but the issue of staff participation in decision making is vital to the question of faculty status. Much
of the older literature emphasizes the hierarchical (in many
cases authoritarian might be as accurate) structure in library
management. Recently, librarians have become more concerned about participation in library government. This
would seem to be an auspicious trend and probably stems
from the rising educational preparation of librarians and
hopefully from a greater concern with the quality of service.
Also, on the purely practical level, if librarians have no
voice in the affairs of their own unit, why should they seek
a voice in faculty government?

As has often been indicated, the educational level of
librarians has risen considerably since 1900. It is, however, not clear whether this reflects a cause or effect relationship as far as faculty status is concerned. That is, have
librarians increasingly gained faculty status as they bring a
higher level of education to their jobs, or are librarians
pursuing additional formal study because having faculty status
places greater pressure upon them to emulate the faculty
with whom they are identified? Possibly it works in both
ways. It seems unlikely that librarians will gain acceptance
unless they have a minimal level of preparation. Once they
have gained faculty status they are under pressure to upgrade
their credentials for the sake of meeting criteria for promotion. This is strongly suggested by the comments of a number of respondents. A more detailed study of this phenomo-
non might be of value.

The concept of applying censure and sanctions against
institutions which treat librarians unfairly is gaining support
from librarians, and that may be the only alternative in some

instances.   However, when using this approach, librarians must remember that the appointment, promotion, and tenure of faculty members in many institutions involves having the doctorate or a creditable scholarly record, or both the degree and the scholarly record.   To argue that as many librarians as faculty members should hold the rank of professor or associate professor is to demand preferential treatment unless both groups present equal credentials.   If librarians persist in ignoring these facts, they do so at their own risk.

The writer believes that faculty status for librarians is essential.   Unless the librarian has an opportunity to participate fully in the educational enterprise, he will be less capable of rendering the quality of service required.   On a long term basis this would also seem to be the best way to improve the qualifications of librarians; for when they are closely identified with the faculty, librarians will also be more likely to adopt (or be forced to adopt) faculty standards for appointment, promotion, and tenure.   In the final analysis, the fact that faculty status for librarians probably has led, and in all likelihood will lead, to continuing pressure on librarians to upgrade their qualifications may be the most cogent reason for supporting faculty status for librarians. Thus one might argue that those faculty members who question the erudition of librarians should be the first to support granting faculty status to librarians.

As far as the present survey is concerned, a preliminary inspection of the results would indicate that the librarians in these 19 institutions do not have full faculty status because: (1) their average salaries were lower; (2) a smaller proportion of them were in the higher academic ranks; (3) they were less likely to receive research funds; and (4) 75 (33.5%) were on annual appointments rather than on academic year contracts.

When taken as a total sample, the librarians were less likely to be in the higher academic ranks, and they received a lower average salary than the faculty members. However, these institutions reward those with the doctorate; and if their credentials are considered, the librarians would seem to receive equitable treatment in both salaries and academic rank.   In fact, the librarians have an advantage over the faculty in that librarians have a greater opportunity to be promoted to the higher academic ranks without the doctorate than have the faculty members.

That librarians are less likely to receive funds for research may be related to the fact that fewer of them engage in this activity than do faculty members. The librarians were more likely to receive travel funds than were faculty members, and speculation would suggest that librarians could get as much research assistance if they considered it important enough.

While it is difficult to assign a precise value to having academic year contracts, this insures longer vacations, which should be a major benefit. Although results were not statistically significant at the .05 level, it may be something of a surprise that a larger percentage of the librarians on 12-month contracts published and anticipated earning another degree. Thus, contrary to assertions in the literature, the term of contract, at least for the librarians who responded in this survey, was not a hindrance to advanced study and scholarly activity.

In summary, many recent surveyors suggest that librarians have met the requirements of faculty status but that they have not received rewards commensurate with their contributions. Drawing comparisons with the literature of other disciplines shows that librarians have not met faculty standards in certain vital areas; this can be documented most easily with regard to academic degrees. Studies show that a larger percentage of faculty members have the doctorate than is true for librarians. Insofar as the results of the present survey are consistent with conditions in other colleges and universities in the United States, the intimations that librarians meet faculty standards for appointment, promotion, and tenure are wishful thinking rather than fact, and the concomitant assertion that librarians receive inequitable treatment is also debatable. If both the responsibilities and benefits of faculty status are considered, the librarians in these 19 institutions enjoy a status which is approximately commensurate with their qualifications and contributions.

Undoubtedly the librarians in these 19 institutions have far better credentials than their predecessors of 30 or 40 years ago. In general, the incumbents enjoy a comparatively high status. It seems safe to conclude that as their educational level and scholarly activity continues to rise, so also will their status in the academic community. Although not intended as a sociological investigation, the results of the survey tend to conform to the findings of sociologists, which indicate that the prestige of a profession is consistent with

the academic preparation and contributions of the practitioners.

SELECTED BIBLIOGRAPHY

Books

Books

American Library Association, Board on Personnel Administration. Classification and Pay Plans for Libraries in Institutions of Higher Education. Vol. 3: Universities. 2nd ed. Chicago: American Library Association, 1947.

American Library Association, Personnel Publications Committee. Personnel Organization and Procedure: A Manual Suggested for Use in College and University Libraries. 2nd ed. Chicago: American Library Association, 1968.

Barber, Bernard. Social Stratification: A Comparative Analysis of Structure and Process. New York: Harcourt, Brace & World, Inc., 1957.

Bendix, Reinhard, and Lipset, Seymour, ed. Class, Status, and Power: Social Stratification in Comparative Perspective. 2nd ed. New York: Free Press, 1966.

Berelson, Bernard. Graduate Education in the United States. New York: McGraw-Hill Book Company, Inc., 1960.

Brown, David G. Academic Labor Markets. Chapel Hill, N. C.: 1965.

Downs, Robert B., ed. The Status of American College and University Librarians. ACRL Monograph, No. 22. Chicago: American Library Association, 1958.

Hall, Anna C. Selected Educational Objectives for Public Service Librarians: A Taxonomic Approach. University of Pittsburgh, 1968.

Heim, Peggy and Cameron, Donald F. The Economics of Librarianship in College and University Libraries, 1969-70: A Sample Survey of Compensations. Washington, D. C.: Council on Library Resources, Inc., 1970.

212

Ingraham, Mark H. The Mirror of Brass: The Compensa-
tion and Working Conditions of College and University
Administrators. Madison: University of Wisconsin
Press, 1968.

_____. The Outer Fringe: Faculty Benefits Other Than An-
nuities and Insurance. Madison: University of Wisconsin Press, 1965.

Lyle, Guy R. The Administration of the College Library.
3rd ed. New York: H. W. Wilson Company, 1961.

_____. The President, the Professor, and the College Li-
brary. New York: H. W. Wilson Company, 1963.

Morrison, Perry D. The Career of the Academic Librarian: A Study of the Social Origins, Educational Attainments, Vocational Experience, and Personality Characteristics of a Group of American Academic Librarians. ACRL Monograph, No. 29. Chicago: American
Library Association, 1969.

Pfnister, Allan O. A Report on the Baccalaureate Origins
of College Faculties. Washington, D. C.: Association
of American Colleges, 1961.

Randall, William M. The College Library: A Descriptive
Study of the Libraries in Four-Year Liberal Arts Colleges in the United States. Chicago: American Library Association, 1932.

Randall, William M., and Goodrich, Francis L. D. Principles of College Library Administration. 2nd ed.
Chicago: American Library Association, 1941.

Reader, W. J. Professional Men: The Rise of the Professional Classes in Nineteenth-Century England. New
York: Basic Books, Inc., 1966.

Schiller, Anita R. Characteristics of Professional Personnel in College and University Libraries. Research
Series, No. 16. Springfield: Illinois State Library,
1969.

Stone, Elizabeth W. Factors Related to the Professional Development of Librarians. Metuchen, N. J.: Scarecrow
Press, Inc., 1969.

U. S. Department of Health, Education, and Welfare, Office
of Education. Sabbatical Leave in American Higher
Education: Origin, Early History, and Current Practices, by Walter C. Eells and Ernest V. Hollis.
Bulletin 1962, No. 17. Washington, D. C.: Government Printing Office, 1962.

Wallin, Herman. Faculty Input: A Function of a College's
Incentive System. Eugene: Center for the Advanced
Study of Educational Administration, University of
Oregon, 1966.

Williams, Robert L. The Administration of Academic Affairs in Higher Education. Ann Arbor: The University of Michigan Press, 1965.

Wilson, Logan. The Academic Man: A Study in the Sociology
of a Profession. New York: Oxford University Press,
1942.

Wilson, Louis R., and Tauber, Maurice F. The University
Library: The Organization, Administration, and Func-
tions of Academic Libraries. 2nd ed. New York:
Columbia University Press, 1956.

Woodburne, Lloyd S. Principles of College and University
Administration. Stanford, Calif.: Stanford University
Press, 1958.

Works, George A. College and University Library Problems:
A Study of a Selected Group of Institutions Prepared
for the Association of American Universities. Chicago:
American Library Association, 1927.

Articles

"Academic Freedom and Tenure: 1940 Statement of Principles." AAUP Bulletin, 53 (Summer, 1957), 246-47.

"Atlantic City Conference: A Great Show in Two Parts and a
Cast of Thousands." ALA Bulletin, 63 (July-August,
1969), 915-64.

"Berkeley Library Union States Bargaining Terms." Library
Journal, 93 (October 15, 1968), 3736.

Bergen, Daniel P. "Librarians and the Bipolarization of the Academic Enterprise. " College and Research Libraries, 24 (November, 1963), 467-80.

Blackburn, Robert T. "College Libraries--Indicted Failures: Some Reasons--and a Possible Remedy. " College and Research Libraries, 29 (May, 1968), 171-77.

Blake, Fay M. "Tenure for the Academic Librarian. " College and Research Libraries, 29 (November, 1968), 502-504.

Blankenship, W. C. "Head Librarians: How Many Men? How Many Women?" College and Research Libraries, 28 (January, 1967), 41-48.

Boughter, Vivian R. "Salaries, Work Week, Vacations, Benefits, and Privileges of College Librarians. " College and Research Libraries, 19 (March, 1958), 126-28.

Branscomb, Lewis C. "Tenure for Professional Librarians on Appointment at Colleges and Universities. " College and Research Libraries, 26 (July, 1965), 297-98, 341.

Bundy, Mary L. , and Wasserman, Paul. "Professionalism Reconsidered. " College and Research Libraries, 29 (January, 1968), 5-26.

Byrd, Cecil K. "Subject Specialists in a University Library." College and Research Libraries, 27 (May, 1966), 191-93.

Caldwell, John. "Degrees Held by Head Librarians of Colleges and Universities. " College and Research Libraries, 23 (May, 1962), 227-28, 260.

Cartter, Allan M. "A New Look at the Supply of College Teachers. " Educational Record, 46 (Summer, 1965), 267-77.

Cassata, Mary B. "Teach-in: The Academic Librarian's Key to Status?" College and Research Libraries, 31 (January, 1970), 22-27.

Coen, George. "Tenure for Librarians. " Library Journal, 91 (January 15, 1966), 212-13.

A Committee of the University of Miami Chapter of the AAUP. "Academic Freedom: Tenure Is Not Enough." AAUP Bulletin, 53 (Summer, 1967), 202-209.

Danton, J. Periam. "Doctoral Study in Librarianship in the United States. " College and Research Libraries, 20 (November, 1959), 435-53, 58.

Downs, Robert B. "The Place of Librarians in Colleges and Universities. " North Carolina Libraries, 18 (Winter, 1960), 34-41.

_____. "Status of Academic Librarians in Retrospect. " College and Research Libraries, 29 (July, 1968), 253-58.

_____. "Status of University Librarians--1964. " College and Research Libraries, 25 (July, 1964), 253-58.

Emerson, William L. "Why Not Try?" Wilson Library Bulletin, 43 (December, 1968), 367-70.

"Essentials in the Training of University Librarians. " College and Research Libraries, 1 (December, 1939), 13-38.

"Financial Value of the Ph. D. for College Faculty Members." NEA Research Bulletin, 44 (October, 1966), 82-84.

Fischer, John. "Is There a Teacher on the Faculty?" Harper's Magazine, February, 1965, pp. 18-28.

Forgotson, Jane. "A Staff Librarian Views the Problem of Status. " College and Research Libraries, 22 (July, 1961), 275-81, 306.

Francis, Roy G. "Publication and Academic Merit. " Modern Language Journal, 51 (November, 1967), 391-94.

Harlow, Neal. "Doctoral Study--Key to What?" College and Research Libraries, 29 (November, 1968), 483-85.

Harvey, John F. "Advancement in the Library Profession. " Wilson Library Bulletin, 36 (October, 1961), 144-47.

Henry, W. E. "The Academic Standing of College Library Assistants and Their Relation to the Carnegie Foundation." Bulletin of the American Library Association, 5 (July, 1911), 258-63.

Hintz, Carl. "Criteria for Appointment to and Promotion in Academic Rank." College and Research Libraries, 29 (September, 1968), 341-46.

Holbrook, Florence. "The Faculty Image of the Academic Librarian." Southeastern Librarian, 18 (Fall, 1968), 174-93.

Houle, Cyril O. "The Role of Continuing Education in Current Professional Development." ALA Bulletin, 61 (March, 1967), 259-67.

"In Defense of the Professor." Journal of Higher Education, 36 (June, 1965), 339-42.

"Is Librarianship a Profession?" California Librarian, 25 (July, 1964), 163-65.

Jesse, William H., and Mitchell, Ann E. "Professional Staff Opportunities for Study and Research." College and Research Libraries, 29 (March, 1968), 87-100.

Jones, Harold D. "LACUNY: A Library Association in Action." California Librarian, 29 (July, 1968), 204-209.

Kellam, W. Porter, and Barker, Dale L. "Activities and Opportunities of University Librarians for Full Participation in the Educational Enterprise." College and Research Libraries, 29 (May, 1968), 195-99.

Kirkpatrick, Leonard H. "Another Approach to Staff Status." College and Research Libraries, 8 (July, 1947), 218-20.

Kraus, Joe W. "The Qualifications of University Librarians, 1948 and 1933." College and Research Libraries, 11 (January, 1950), 17-21.

Lancour, Harold. "The Librarian's Search for Status." Library Quarterly, 31 (October, 1961), 369-81.

"Librarians' Degrees: A Symposium." College and Research Libraries, 6 (June, 1945), 264-78.

McAnally, Arthur M. "Privileges and Obligations of Academic Status.". College and Research Libraries, 24 (March, 1963), 102-108.

McMillen, James A. "Academic Status of Library Staff Members of Large Universities." College and Research Libraries, 1 (March, 1940), 138-40.

Madan, Raj; Hetler, Eliese; and Strong, Marilyn. "The Status of Librarians in Four-Year State Colleges and Universities." College and Research Libraries, 29 (September, 1968), 381-86.

Maloy, Miriam C. "Faculty Status of College Librarians." ALA Bulletin, 33 (April, 1939), 232-33, 302.

Marchant, Maurice P. "Faculty--Librarian Conflict." Library Journal, 94 (September 1, 1969), 2886-89.

Maul, Ray C. "A Look at the New College Teacher." Educational Record, 46 (Summer, 1965), 259-66.

Moriarty, John H. "Academic In Deed." College and Research Libraries, 31 (January, 1970), 14-17.

Morris, Leslie R. "Types of Library Degrees: An Attitude Survey." Journal of Education for Librarianship, 10 (Summer, 1969), 28-32.

Muller, Robert H. "The Research Mind in Library Education and Practice." Library Journal, 92 (March 15, 1967), 1126-29.

Naegele, Kaspar D. and Stolar, Elaine. "Income and Prestige." Library Journal, 85 (September 1, 1960), 2888-91.

Naegele, Kaspar D., and Stolar, Elaine. "The Librarian of the Northwest." Pacific Northwest Library Association. Library Development Project Reports. Vol. 4: Libraries and Librarians of the Pacific Northwest. Edited by Morton Kroll. Seattle: University of Washington Press, 1960, pp. 51-137.

Orlich, Donald C. "Universities and the Generation of Knowledge." Education, 88 (September-October, 1967), 82-86.

218

Perreault, Jean M. "What Is 'Academic Status?'" College and Research Libraries, 27 (May, 1966), 207-10, 232.

Pollard, Frances M. "Characteristics of Negro College Chief Librarians." College and Research Libraries, 25 (July, 1964), 281-84.

Pope, Mary F. and Thompson, Lawrence S. "Travel Funds for University Library Staffs." College and Research Libraries, 11 (January, 1950), 22-27.

Posey, Edwin D. "The Librarian and the Faculty." Southeastern Librarian, 18 (Fall, 1968), 152-61.

Sable, Arnold P. "The Sexuality of the Library Profession: The Male and Female Librarian." Wilson Library Bulletin, 43 (April, 1969), 748-51.

Schmitt, Hans A. "Teaching and Research: Companions or Adversaries?" Journal of Higher Education, 36 (November, 1965), 419-27.

Seibert, Russel H. "Status and Responsibilities of Academic Librarians." College and Research Libraries, 22 (July, 1961), 253-55.

Slavens, Thomas P. "Opinions of Library Science Phd's about Requirements for the PhD's Degree in Library Science." College and Research Libraries, 30 (November, 1969), 525-32.

Smith, Eldred. "Academic Status for College and University Librarians--Problems and Prospects." College and Research Libraries, 31 (January, 1970), 7-13.

Spain, Frances L. "Faculty Status of Librarians in Colleges and Universities of the South." Southeastern Library Association. Papers and Proceedings. 13th Biennial Conference, Louisville, Ky., October 20-23, 1948, pp. 45-53.

"Standards for College Libraries." College and Research Libraries, 20 (July, 1959), 274-80.

"A Statement on Leaves of Absence." AAUP Bulletin, 53 (Autumn, 1967), 270-74.

"Status of Academic Librarians in California. " California Librarian, 29 (January, 1968), 37-39.

"Status of California State College Librarians. " American Libraries, 1 (January, 1970), 57-59.

"Status of College and University Librarians. " College and Research Libraries, 20 (September, 1959), 399-400.

"Status of College Librarians in Texas. " Library Journal, 76 (March 15, 1951), 500-501.

Stieg, Lewis F. "Retirement Plans for College and University Librarians. " College and Research Libraries, 11 (January, 1950), 10-16.

Stinchcombe, Arthur L. , ed. "A Kaleidoscopic View of Library Research. " Wilson Library Bulletin, 41 (May, 1967), 896-949.

"Tenure in Libraries: A Statement of Principles Adopted by the Council of the American Library Association, June 21, 1946. " ALA Bulletin, 40 (November, 1946), 451-53.

"The University Librarian as Bookman and Administrator: A Symposium. " College and Research Libraries, 15 (July, 1954), 313-31.

Veit, Fritz. "The Status of the Librarian According to Accrediting Standards of Regional and Professional Associations. " College and Research Libraries, 21 (March, 1960), 127-35.

Vosper, Robert. "Needed: An Open End Career Policy: A Critique of Classification and Pay Plans for Libraries. " ALA Bulletin, 56 (October, 1962), 833-35.

Weber, David C. "'Tenure' for Librarians in Academic Institutions. " College and Research Libraries, 27 (March, 1966), 99-102.

Woodring, Paul. "The Profession of College Teaching. " Journal of Higher Education, 31 (May, 1960), 180-82.

Unpublished Material

Adair, Fred. "The Development of a Scale to Measure the Service Orientation of Librarians: Preliminary Investigations. " Unpublished Ph. D. dissertation, University of North Carolina, 1968.

Blankenship, Winson. "Attitudes of Head Librarians toward Some Aspects of College Librarianship. " Unpublished Ed. D. dissertation, Oklahoma State University, 1963.

Blayton, Reida. "A Study of the Characteristics of Professional Catalogers as Indicated in Who's Who in Library Service, 1955. " Unpublished Master's thesis, Atlanta University, 1960.

Bradley, Ben W. "A Study of the Characteristics, Qualifications, and Succession Patterns of Heads of Large United States Academic and Public Libraries. " Unpublished Master's report, University of Texas, 1968.

Byles, Tony B. "A Status Study of Teachers in Selected Colleges of Education in Louisiana. " Unpublished Ed. D. dissertation, University of Southern Mississippi, 1963.

Carrington, Dorothy. "An Analysis of Factors Affecting the Decison of College Women Seniors of the Southeast to Enter Graduate School. " Unpublished Ed. D. dissertation, Florida State University, 1961.

Farley, Delbert R. "The Image of the College Professor as Disclosed in General Magazines, 1938-1963. " Unpublished Ph. D. dissertation, Florida State University, 1964.

Farley, Richard A. "The American Library Executive: An Inquiry into His Concepts of the Functions of His Office. " Unpublished Ph. D. dissertation, University of Illinois, 1967.

Hakanson, Eugene. "The College Professor, 1946-1965, as Revealed by an Analysis of Selected Magazine Articles. " Unpublished Ed. D. dissertation, Indiana University, 1967.

Knox, Margaret. "Professional Development of Reference
    Librarians in a University Library: A Case Study."
    Unpublished Ph. D. thesis, University of Illinois, 1957.

Mackey, Harold F. "A Study of the Prestige Associated with
    Selected Expectations Held for Members of the Resi-
    dent Instructional Staff in a Land-Grant University."
    Unpublished Ph. D. dissertation, Washington State Uni-
    versity, 1965.

Meyer, Donald P. "An Investigation of Perceptions Regard-
    ing the Instructional Function of the Library among
    Faculty Members and Librarians at Public Community
    Colleges in Michigan." Unpublished Ed. D. disserta-
    tion, Michigan State University, 1968.

Nandi, Proshanta K. "Career and Life Organization of Pro-
    fessionals: A Study of Contrasts between College and
    University Professors." Unpublished Ph. D. disserta-
    tion, University of Minnesota, 1968.

Parrott, Shirley. "An Analysis of the Biographies of Li-
    brarians Listed in Who's Who of American Women,
    1958-1959." Unpublished Master's thesis, Atlanta
    University, 1962.

Phoenix, William D. "The Doctorate and the University Li-
    brary Administrator." Unpublished Ph. D. disserta-
    tion, University of Missouri at Kansas City, 1965.

Pollard, Frances M. "Characteristics of Negro College
    Chief Librarians." Unpublished Ph. D. dissertation,
    Western Reserve University, 1963.

Rockafellow, Theodore F. "The Philosophy, Purpose, and
    Function of Tenure Legislation." Unpublished Ed. D.
    dissertation, Colorado State College, 1967.

Scherer, Henry H. "Faculty-Librarian Relationships in Se-
    lected Liberal Arts Colleges." Unpublished Ed. D.
    dissertation, University of Southern California, 1960.

Schufletowski, Frank W. "The Development of the College
    Professor's Image in the United States from 1946-
    1964." Unpublished Ph. D. dissertation, Washington
    State University, 1966.

Seeliger, Ronald A. "Librarians in <u>Who's Who in America</u>, 1956-1957. " Unpublished Master's thesis, University of Texas, 1961.

Williams, Donald T. , Jr. "The Concepts, Status and Role, as They Affect the Study of Higher Education. " Unpublished Ph. D. dissertation, Stanford University, 1963.

Zimmerman, Lee. "The Academic and Professional Education of College and University Librarians. " Unpublished Master's thesis, University of Illinois, 1932.

INDEX

Academic freedom 98-101
Academic rank, See Rank, academic
Academic status, See Faculty status
Age
 of librarians 73
 of survey respondents 113-15
Appointments, criteria for 2, 31-32, 44-47, 85-87, 197
 See also Contract, term of

Benefits of faculty status, See Committees, service on;
 Contract, term of; Leaves; Publication and research,
 time and funds for; Rank, academic; Salaries; Tenure;
 Travel funds

Chief librarian
 attitudes toward faculty status 21-23, 31-32
 education of 52-55, 128-29
 publication and research of 63, 142
 rank of 85-86, 94, 157-58
 salaries of 92, 94-95, 97
 sex of 70-71, 117
 status of 15-20
 survey respondents 117
Classification of librarians, See Rank, academic
Colleges and universities in the survey 6
Committees, service on 63-65, 143-48
Contract, term of 103
 as related to educational aspirations of librarians 176-78
 as related to publication and research 175-177

Degrees, academic, See education

Education
 as related to
  publication and research 141-42
  rank 93-97, 155-58, 169, 171-72
  salary 95-96, 166-72
  sex 71-73, 126-32 passim

225

status 11-12, 43-47
comments by faculty and librarians on requirements 43-
  49, 133-38, 184-85, 190-93
incentives for 56, 58-60
minimal requirements for librarians 43-49, 133-38
of survey respondents 126-31
pressure to work toward doctorate 131-33
previous surveys
  of faculty members 56-57
  of librarians 49-56
Experience
  as required qualification 46
  of survey respondents 115-18

Faculty benefits, See Benefits of faculty status
Faculty members
  in present survey 6-7, 112-13
  relations with librarians 23-33 passim
  status of 25-26, 60-61
  See also Education, Publication and research, Salaries,
    etc.
Faculty rank, See Rank, academic
Faculty status of librarians
  attitudes toward 1-2, 21-33, 186-90
  benefits of 1-3, 85
    See also Committees, service on; Contract, term of;
      Leaves; Publication and research, time and funds
      for; Rank, academic; Salaries; Tenure; Travel
      funds
  comments on by survey respondents
    faculty members 185-88, 197
    librarians 189-95, 197
  conflicts resulting from 23-33 passim
  definition of 5, 11-14
  historical survey of 3-5, 15-21
  kind of status sought by librarians 21-23
  librarians ranked among ten academic positions 120,
    122-24, 185-88, 195-96
  reasons for seeking
    as means of gaining faculty benefits 31-33
    as means of providing opportunity for better service
      26-31
    for its own sake and social status 23-26
  related literature, importance of 3-5, 43
  responsibilities of 2-3, 43
  See also Committees, service on; Education; Pro-
    fessional activities; Publication and research
    See also Status

226

Funds for publication and research, See Publication and
    research, time and funds for

Government, academic, See Participation in academic
    government

Head librarian, See Chief librarian

Leaves
    definition of 87
    of survey respondents 159-64, 194, 197
    previous surveys of 88-91
Librarians
    for benefits and responsibilities of faculty status, See
        Education; Publication and research; Rank, academic;
        Salaries, etc.
    in present survey 5-7, 112-13
        position of 117-20
        supervisory responsibilities of 120-21
        See also Age, Experience, Teaching
Librarians' rank among ten academic positions 120, 122-24,
    185-88, 195-96
Library government, participation in by librarians 99-102

Meetings, professional, See Professional activities

Participation in academic government 63-65, 100-02, 143-48
Professional activities 65-66, 148-52
Professions, status of 11-12, 25-26
Publication and research 60-63, 102-03, 138-42
    as related to
        education 141-42
        rank, academic 60-61
        salaries 63, 172-73
        sex 63, 140, 142, 153-54, 173
        status 60-63
        time and funds for 62-63, 102-03, 178-80
    importance of 60-62
Purpose of the study 3

Questions investigated 7-8

Rank, academic 85-87, 155-59, 172
    as related to
        education 86, 95-96, 155-58, 169, 171-72
        publication and research 86-87, 172-73
        salaries 93-97 passim, 169-72
        sex 158
227

of chief librarians 85-86, 94, 157
Respondents, description and general characteristics of
6-7, 112-13
See also Age; Experience; Sample, description of; Supervisory responsibilities (librarians only); Teaching load
Responsibilities of faculty status, See Committees, service
on; Education; Professional activities; Publication and
research

Sabbatical leaves, See Leaves
Salaries 92-97, 164-73
as related to
education 97-98, 186-70
publication and research 172-73
rank, academic 93-97, 169, 171-72
sex 67-68, 72, 154, 156-68
historical survey of 92-97
of chief librarians 94-97
Sample
description of 5-7, 112-13
institutions included 6
Sex 66-73, 152-54, 158, 206
as related to
education 71-73, 166-70
position 68-71, 117, 119
publication and research 63, 72, 140, 142, 153-54
rank, academic 71, 93-97, 158
salary 67-68, 72, 154, 166-73
supervisory responsibilities 120-21
historical survey of 66-73
of survey respondents 113
See also Education; Publication and research; Rank,
academic; Salaries, etc.
Status
as related to education 11-12, 43-47
definition of 11-12
of faculty members 25-26
of librarians See Faculty status
Study
definition of terms and limitations of 5-7
methodology 7
need for 2-3
purpose of 3
Supervisory responsibilities of librarians 120-21
Survey
description of 5-7
methodology 7
related literature, importance of 3-5, 43

Teaching load of respondents 124-25
Tenure 97-102, 174-75, 183, 194
    definition of 97
    importance of
        for faculty members 98-99, 101
        for librarians 99-102
Term of contract, See Contract, term of
Time for research, See Publication and research, time
    and funds for
Travel funds 103-04, 181-82

Universities and colleges in the survey 6

Vacation, See Contract, term of
Voting privileges, See Participation in academic govern-
    ment